# Launching a Capital Facility Project:
## A Guide for Healthcare Leaders, Second Edition

---

Your board, staff, or clients may also benefit from this book's insight. For more information on quantity discounts, contact the Health Administration Press Marketing Manager at (312) 424–9470.

This publication is intended to provide accurate and authoritative information in regard to the subject matter covered. It is sold, or otherwise provided, with the understanding that the publisher is not engaged in rendering professional services. If professional advice or other expert assistance is required, the services of a competent professional should be sought.

The statements and opinions contained in this book are strictly those of the author and do not represent the official positions of the American College of Healthcare Executives or the Foundation of the American College of Healthcare Executives.

Copyright © 2010 by the Foundation of the American College of Healthcare Executives. Printed in the United States of America. All rights reserved. This book or parts thereof may not be reproduced in any form without written permission of the publisher.

15  14  13  12  11    5  4  3  2  1

**Library of Congress Cataloging-in-Publication Data**

Kemper, John E.
  Launching a Capital Facility Project : a guide for healthcare leaders / John Kemper. — 2nd ed.
    p. ; cm.
  Rev. ed. of: Launching a healthcare capital project /John Kemper. c2004.
  Includes bibliographical references.
  ISBN 978-1-56793-359-8 (alk. paper)
  1. Health facilities—Planning. 2. Strategic planning. 3. Hospital administrators. I. Kemper, John E. Launching a healthcare capital project. II. Title.
  [DNLM: 1. Health Facility Planning—organization & administration. 2. Health Facility Administrators.
3. Planning Techniques. WX 140 K32p 2010]
  RA967.K43 2010
  068'2—dc22
                                                                    2010000268

The paper used in this publication meets the minimum requirements of American National Standard for Information Sciences—Permanence of Paper for Printed Library Materials, ANSI Z39.48-1984. ⊚™

Acquisitions editor: Eileen Lynch; Project manager: Dojna Shearer; Cover designer: Daniel Rodriguez; Layout: BookComp

Cover photo of Atrium Medical Center used by permission.

Found an error or a typo? We want to know! Please e-mail it to hap1@ache.org, and put "Book Error" in the subject line.

For photocopying and copyright information, please contact Copyright Clearance Center at www.copyright.com or at (978) 750–8400.

Health Administration Press
A division of the Foundation of the American
   College of Healthcare Executives
One North Franklin Street, Suite 1700
Chicago, IL 60606–3529
(312) 424–2800

# Introduction

Since the first edition of this book was published in 2004, many changes have occurred that have affected the delivery of healthcare capital projects. Capital projects implemented by healthcare owners have become fewer and smaller in scope. With the collapse of the capital markets in late 2008, many healthcare owners placed their capital projects on hold and substantially reduced the scope of projects that moved forward. This reduction in the number and size of projects presents a tremendous opportunity to substantially improve the implementation of healthcare capital projects. Over more than three decades of assisting healthcare owners in the successful delivery of their capital projects, I have seen numerous disorganized and ineffective processes. Many projects were started and managed by dysfunctional teams, resulting in wasted resources. Completed projects were seen as total failures because of cost and schedule overruns and, more importantly, because they did not substantially improve operational efficiency, the patient experience, or the delivery of healthcare services. Project teams experienced a range of emotions including enthusiasm, disillusionment, panic, encouragement, anger, and relief. Starting and implementing a capital facility project does not have to be this way. Devising a structured and collaborative process at the onset can minimize emotional swings and keep the project on track.

This book provides healthcare owners and their boards a roadmap for productive and rewarding project delivery. It discusses the intricacies of the delivery process, the pitfalls to avoid, and the importance of assembling a complete and experienced delivery team. As was the case with the first edition of this book, the Project Launch Phase is emphasized. A new tool to begin this phase will also be introduced. **Launch Gap Analysis**, discussed in Chapter 2, is the most important step in successful project delivery. Bridging the strategic plan phase and the design phase, the launch phase defines the project and gives the organization a chance to make changes with a minimal investment of funds. Launch Gap Analysis is the key to a successful launch. ▶

In any complex undertaking, the end depends on the beginning. Healthcare executives charged with such a multifaceted undertaking as a capital project must develop their skills in launching, organizing, and implementing. Lack of such a skill base jeopardizes the organization's investments in time, money, and human resources. Getting it right the first time is critical. Effective use and management of capital expenditures improves the organization's ability to deliver healthcare services now and far into the future. It affects not only healthcare consumers but also the organization's staff and communities.

The specific benefits of this book to each functional level of responsibility are as follows:

- **For CEOs and senior management:** This book serves as a framework, defining the key components of the project delivery process, the expected outcomes, and the risks involved.
- **For board members:** This book is a guide to optimizing capital expenditures, from the strategic planning phase through the transition and occupancy phase.
- **For medical staff members:** This book details how physician and clinical staff input and perspectives contribute to the improvement of healthcare delivery.
- **For the project delivery team:** This book identifies members' roles and responsibilities during the launch phase and explains how their involvement affects project implementation.
- **For employees:** This book defines the staff's role in identifying workflow improvements and operational efficiencies necessary to ensure that the completed facility improves the patient experience.
- **For all stakeholders involved in delivering a capital project:** This book explains the importance of the launch gap analysis, the first and most critical step in the successful delivery of capital projects, and introduces a new and innovative delivery approach known as integrated project delivery (IPD) that has the potential to radically improve the method of project delivery for all project delivery team members.

With guidance and planning, a healthcare owner can provide an outstanding facility designed to best meet the immediate and future healthcare needs of the community in a cost-effective and operationally efficient manner.

# CHAPTER 1

# Phases of the Project Delivery Process

## AN INTEGRATED DELIVERY PROCESS IS THE KEY TO THE OVERALL SUCCESS OF THE PROJECT.

This chapter provides an overview of the five phases of the delivery process. These phases are interrelated. Each phase ends in the achievement of a major work product (see Exhibit 1.1). Decisions made in one phase affect the other phases. Therefore, all aspects of the total delivery process, from strategic plan to transition and occupancy, must be integrated. The project team must not proceed to the next phase before achieving the work product for the current phase and gaining approval from all key stakeholders.

Following a structured and collaborative process can reduce or eliminate most, if not all, of the following problems:

- Unclear need and scope
- Poor land acquisition decisions
- Uncertain budget and schedule ▶

## Exhibit 1.1: Capital Delivery Process

| Strategic Plan Phase | Project Launch Phase | Design Phase | Construction Phase | Transition and Occupancy Phase |
|---|---|---|---|---|
| • Mission/vision creation<br>• Internal assessment<br>• External assessment<br>• Medical staff assessment<br>• Regulatory controls assessment<br>• Delivery model identification<br>• Strategies/initiatives identification<br>• Strategic financial plan establishment<br>• Debt capacity analysis<br>• Identification of capital facility needs | • Strategic master facilities plan<br>• Project visioning and guiding principles<br>• Site analysis and land acquisition<br>• Project delivery approach<br>• Project delivery team organization<br>• Alternative financing opportunities<br>• Integrated process planning<br>• Master program budget and scheduling<br>• Medical technology and equipment strategy<br>• Regulatory approval process<br>• Transition and occupancy strategy | • Schematic design<br>• Design development<br>• Mock-ups of key clinical areas<br>• Construction documents<br>• Medical equipment and technology planning<br>• Master project budget and schedule refinement<br>• Value analysis<br>• Operations integration and implementation<br>• Transition readiness assessment | • Mobilization and start-up<br>• Kick-off and stakeholders expectations session<br>• Development of quality control plan<br>• Project construction<br>• Equipment delivery, installation, and testing<br>• Building commissioning<br>• Inspections/certifications<br>• Coordination with ongoing operations<br>• Detailed transition and occupancy planning | • Staff training/orientation<br>• FF&E installation<br>• Move day management<br>• Staff and patient occupancy<br>• Post occupancy audit |
| **Product:**<br>Strategic master facility plan | **Products:**<br>Launch Gap Analysis<br>Project implementation plan | **Products:**<br>Final construction contract, final program budget and schedule, transition gap analysis | **Products:**<br>Completed facility<br>Certificate of occupancy | **Product:**<br>Functioning facility |

- Costs that exceed debt capacity
- Slow and frustrating design process
- Community and board confusion about scope, costs, and goals
- Low user satisfaction
- Difficult construction process
- Adverse effects on ongoing operations
- Operational inefficiencies in the new facility

## STRATEGIC PLAN PHASE

Before launching a project, clear strategic and financial guidelines must be established. Projects initiated without this basis can quickly get out of control. In the strategic planning phase, a comprehensive plan is created that defines the organization's vision, mission, and strategic market position. The plan also identifies goals and objectives for establishing new services, modifying existing programs or services, and penetrating into new markets. The strategic vision must drive the development of a strategic master facilities plan that integrates the traditional strategic plan, as Exhibit 1.2 shows. This plan should include facilities solutions that support the strategic direction.

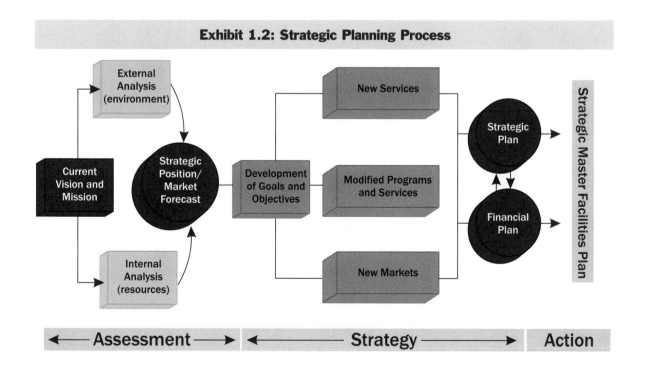

**Exhibit 1.2: Strategic Planning Process**

The strategic master facilities plan becomes the foundation for an organization's capital plan. The word "strategic" is key. To optimize their value, significant facility investments must support strategy, operations, finance, and clinical services. Strategic master facility planning must consider more than architecture and facilities alone.

The strategic master facilities plan should first address any strategic and operational questions that must be answered to appropriately plan for new or expanded facilities. Strategies, operations, clinical efficiencies, and financial capabilities should drive building design, not the other way around.

This phase of the process will not be discussed in detail, but the Suggested Reading list at the end of this book includes several publications that explore the strategic planning phase. Chapter 2 further discusses the development of a strategic master facilities plan.

The strategic master facilities plan integrates strategy, clinical services, operations, finance, and facilities and serves as a road map to effective and efficient delivery of health services. It must be completed and agreed on by all key stakeholders before work on the launch phase can begin.

## PROJECT LAUNCH PHASE

The project launch phase focuses on organization and planning. It sets the project expectations and defines the "Big Three": project scope, budget, and schedule. The chief executive officer (CEO) should drive this phase, assembling and preparing the internal and external delivery teams. Early in the phase, the CEO and key team members should create a project vision and guiding principles that serve as guardrails for the project.

Team members establish a system of checks and balances that will ensure that the strategic master facilities plan and project vision are transformed into a solid project implementation plan. Critical decisions on project scope, budget, and schedule should be made during this phase, because changes at this early stage will have less effect on costs (see Exhibit 1.3).

The most valuable tool during this phase is the Launch Gap Analysis (discussed in detail in Chapter 2). Knowledge gained using this tool becomes the foundation of the project implementation plan—the major work product of this phase—which details the project's scope, cost, and implementation schedule. Prior to the design phase, the project

**Exhibit 1.3: Early Decisions Have a Lesser Effect on Cost**

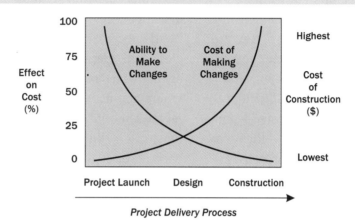

*Project Delivery Process*

implementation plan should be presented to the board for approval and to the community to enlist support.

## DESIGN PHASE

A mistake that delivery teams frequently make is jumping too quickly into the design phase. The team should ensure that expectations about scope, cost, schedule, and final outcome are realistic before the design phase begins.

Form follows function—the 3F theory. Many healthcare planners and architects use this phrase but seldom follow it. Process design/redesign, programming, and schematic design are often poorly aligned at the outset of the design phase. The

traditional model of engaging separate, nonrelated parties must change. A new paradigm is evolving in which an integrated design team is formed early in the process to tackle process flow, space programming, and schematic design at the same time. This integrated process planning dissects the patient experience to define value and eliminate waste. Following this new paradigm in the initial stages will lead to a more efficient and cost-effective design. Integrated process planning will be discussed further in Chapter 2.

At key stages of the design process, the construction manager and the project delivery team complete detailed budget estimates and send them to the delivery team for review and approval. These estimates keep the design development within budget. A common mistake delivery teams make during the design phase is failing to carefully review the budget updates and to require explanations for each cost item. Sufficient review time must be allocated—normally three to four weeks—for each budget update to allow the delivery team to reach a consensus on design changes needed to keep the project within budget. This process prevents cost-related surprises when the final project budget is submitted. Avoiding all surprises is impossible, but involvement of the entire delivery team in design and budgeting results in a smooth process and an optimal construction contract.

Another issue to address during the design phase is the integration of medical technology and equipment into the design. The budgets for equipment and systems alone can represent approximately 20 percent of the total project budget. In addition, technology and equipment needs significantly affect space needs. Therefore, the design team must consider space for equipment in planning the overall design. The cost of this equipment should be an integral part of the budget development and the estimate updates during this phase.

During the design phase, a master project schedule should be developed, reviewed, and approved by the necessary regulatory agencies. Zoning approvals, state health agency reviews, certificates of need where applicable, and environmental reviews should be entered into the master schedule and the budget, as each requires time and money.

The major work products of the design phase are completed construction documents; a final project budget that includes a list of furniture, fixtures, and equipment (FF&E) needed; a transition readiness assessment; and a final construction contract.

## CONSTRUCTION PHASE

This phase will not be discussed in depth in this book, but the Suggested Reading list includes related publications and seminars on this topic.

If the strategic, launch, and design phases are developed properly, the construction phase will be less daunting. A new project delivery process known as integrated project delivery (IPD) has the potential to radically improve the entire process, especially the construction phase. IPD will be discussed in Chapter 4.

Ideally, the delivery team (including internal and external members) has been working collaboratively since the launch phase began. If this is the case, the delivery team, including the construction manager, should understand the project's scope, budget, and schedule and how the construction will affect the ongoing operations of the healthcare organization before construction begins.

A key issue in the construction phase is the coordination, delivery, and installation of medical and technology equipment. Too often these tasks are overlooked—an oversight that can significantly affect the schedule and final cost of the project. Minimize or avert these mistakes by assigning responsibility for them to a member of the delivery team.

The end work products of the construction phase are a certificate of occupancy and a completed facility that is ready to be occupied.

## TRANSITION AND OCCUPANCY PHASE

The most important component of the transition and occupancy phase is development and management of the transition plan. For large and multifaceted projects, planning the transition and occupancy can be as complicated as the design and construction phases. If a major move is necessary (which is often the case in healthcare), the designated transition and occupancy team should begin planning during the design phase by completing a transition readiness assessment (TRA). This document will detail the organization and key responsibilities of the transition and occupancy team, develop the budget and schedule for this phase, and detail the implementation plan. During the construction phase, and no later than 18 to 20 months before the projected occupancy date, the transition and occupancy team should begin planning details and holding regularly scheduled meetings. Move-in should not occur immediately upon completion of the facility. At least 60 days should be allocated between receipt of the certificate of occupancy and the actual move to allow for building commissioning and final staff training.

When executed properly, the transition and occupancy phase is the one most stakeholders will recall because it is the culmination of all the hard work done to make the project a success. Failure at this phase, even if all other phases were successful, will leave a negative impression. It is never too early to begin planning for this phase, so spend sufficient time on it to ensure that the finish is as strong as the start.

## KEY POINTS

Remember the following key points about the overall delivery approach:

- Follow a set, structured, collaborative process for all capital projects.
- The end depends on the beginning, so focus on the beginning (the launch phase).
- Stick to the processes of each phase; do not jump ahead without completing a phase's major work product.
- Develop a comprehensive strategic master facilities plan prior to the launch phase.
- Complete a launch gap analysis which will define the Big Three—scope, budget, and schedule—and align all key stakeholders' expectations upfront.
- Communicate project goals and objectives (the Big Three) to the delivery team prior to the start of design.
- Do not do it alone. Select key delivery team members based on their qualifications and experience with similar healthcare projects.
- Begin the design with integrated process planning, and apply Lean process tools to value stream map key operational processes, eliminate waste, and define the key operational processes to be implemented in the new or expanded facility.
- Implement IPD to involve all the key delivery team members at the start of the process and ensure that the Big Three are controlled from start to finish.
- If a move is involved, complete a TRA and begin detailed planning at least 18 to 20 months before projected occupancy.
- Allow a minimum of 60 days after obtaining a certificate of occupancy before actually moving in. This time gives you an opportunity to sufficiently train staff and complete building commissioning.
- Finish as strong as you started by properly executing the transition and occupancy phase.

# CHAPTER 2

# Project Launch Phase

## THE END DEPENDS ON THE BEGINNING.

The project launch phase is the most critical part of the delivery process, but it is also the least understood. During this phase, the project delivery team is formed (see Chapter 3); the scope, budget, and schedule are defined; and the project implementation plan—the foundation on which the project will be designed and constructed—is established. Healthcare owners must allocate sufficient time for the launch phase and ensure that the design phase does not begin before the launch phase is complete. This will increase the likelihood of success, especially from the cost and schedule perspective. A successfully completed launch phase makes the design, construction, and transition and occupancy phases pleasant and collaborative, rather than adversarial, costly, and frustrating. ▶

## LAUNCH GAP ANALYSIS

The first step to launch phase success is to complete a launch gap analysis. This involves a thorough and rigorous exploration and evaluation of major components of a capital project (the spokes of the wheel in Exhibit 2.1). Conducting a launch gap analysis ensures a comprehensive, well-planned capital project approach that aligns expectations and goals at the outset of the project.

When you hop in your car to take a road trip, do you know the purpose of your journey? Do you have

Exhibit 2.1: Launch Gap Analysis

a map or sufficient directions to get you to your destination? Do you have money in your pocket for food and unexpected expenses? Do you make sure your family is in the car with you? Do you know how long it will take to get where you want to go? Of course you do!

Now, think about embarking on a large-scale capital project, such as a replacement hospital or a major tower addition. Do you have a purpose for the project (strategy)? How about a road map (structured process)? Do you have enough money for expected and unexpected expenses (budget)? Is your "family" (your internal and external project delivery teams) on board? Do you know how long the project will take (schedule)? In short, are you ready to launch? You may be able to answer some of these questions, but probably not all of them. And there may be some questions you have never even considered.

In a launch gap analysis, every major issue that might affect the launch is identified and explored. It is broader and deeper than a visioning exercise focused on major design and building elements. The major phases of the analysis echo a physician's process in treating a patient. They are as follows:

- **Discovery (patient history and physical):** What information is currently available? This involves initial data gathering and pre-session interviews.
- **Gap analysis (diagnosis):** Where are the gaps in knowledge? What additional information is needed? What is already done? What still needs to be completed?
- **Implementation plan (treatment plan):** How can we bridge the gaps to ensure that everyone's expectations are aligned and that we're on the same path?

The launch gap analysis will keep you focused on the elements that impact the Big Three: scope, budget, and schedule. The major project components analyzed during this process are discussed in the following sections.

## Strategic Master Facilities Plan

Developing a realistic and implementable strategic master facilities plan requires a rigorous process (shown in Exhibit 2.2) that addresses the following five key action elements:

1. **Identify tactical elements.** You have defined the strategic need

**Exhibit 2.2: Strategic Master Facilities Plan**

for a facility project. It is now time to develop the *what* of the plan—the organization's needs-and-wants response to internal and external analysis. What is the scope of services the facility will offer?

2. **Define the delivery model.** Once you have defined the scope of services, you must determine how they will be delivered. Address all elements of the patient encounter and the care delivered, including care access, support, delivery, tracking, and accounting.

3. **Assess the physical environment.** A thorough evaluation of the current facilities, the site (existing or "green field"), and the site's physical situation must be conducted, and the desired future state must be determined. Bridging the gap between the current and the envisioned environment will clarify design intent, context, and principles.

4. **Complete a financial analysis.** Address fiscal concerns by calculating how much you can afford to spend, identifying the method

of financing, and determining whether the project is sustainable. An affordable plan that spends the institution's money wisely is a basic fiduciary responsibility.

5. **Understand regulatory controls.** Know what approvals you need and how they may affect your plan. These include zoning/land-use constraints, certificate of need (CON) controls, and permit requirements.

## Project Vision and Guiding Principles

How well do you understand evidence-based design, LEED certification, and sustainable design concepts? What do these concepts mean to your project? What does it mean to be truly flexible? Early in the launch phase, the governing body for the implementation of the project must develop a project vision and guiding principles (see Exhibit 2.3 for an example). This document serves as the initial road map for the project and helps align key stakeholders and create excitement and buy-in for the project among staff, patients, and the community.

## Site Analysis and Land Acquisition

Selecting the right site is a crucial early step. Location is vital, but it is not the only site issue to consider. When inadequate time is allocated for analyzing various land options, the land itself drives the design. To prevent this, the land-acquisition process must, at a minimum, involve consideration of the following factors:

- **Size.** Make sure the land is large enough to meet long-range growth plans—that is, a 10-year to 20-year plan.
- **Usability.** Determine the total acreage that can be used. The total size purchased is rarely the same as the total acres available for the actual building development.
- **Zoning restrictions.** Be aware of the current zoning limitations and allowances for the area. For example, ask whether day care centers, medical office buildings, and retirement and long-term-care facilities are allowed in addition to the hospital.
- **Potential adjacent development.** Find out what businesses and developments are planned or permissible on the adjacent parcels of land. Those potential developments might not be compatible with healthcare delivery.
- **Site access.** Determine whether the site is accessible from major

**Exhibit 2.3: Replacement Hospital Vision and Guiding Principles**

**Vision Statement**
The new hospital campus will be the healthcare destination of choice and will transform the healthcare experience of the hospital community. We will expand our family of exceptional physicians and associates to provide state-of-the-art care and an extraordinary patient experience.

**Guiding Principles**

- Optimize *operational efficiency* through *incorporation of technology,* innovation, and use of best practices.

- Embrace *patient-centered* concepts to support a *healing* environment.

- Embrace *environmentally responsible* design.

- Design a facility that *reflects the care we deliver.*

- Design a facility that *meets the needs of the scope of services* we deliver.

- *Seek associate and physician input* throughout the process.

- *Engage the community* through active communication throughout the process.

- Use *evidence-based design* concepts to *enhance clinical quality and patient safety.*

- Design an *inviting, safe, and customer-friendly* campus.

- Adopt *design flexibility* for future expansion and practice changes.

- *Provide the community with passive recreation* whenever possible.

- Make all decisions within the context of *fiscal responsibility.*

- Develop an *integrated medical arts campus.*

- *Use local resources* whenever possible and appropriate.

- Provide an environment that *enhances the quality of work life* for associates and physicians.

roads and how visible it is to passersby.

- **Services to the site.** Evaluate the cost of bringing service utilities to the site.

- **Preliminary master site plan.** Prepare preliminary master site plans for each potential property. This plan ensures that all cur-

rent planned facilities and their associated parking needs fit the property.

Land acquisition is one area where the healthcare owner needs external help. Typically, the healthcare owner hires a local real estate firm. This approach works if the real estate firm employs an agent with experience in assisting healthcare organizations through the land-acquisition process and who knows the ramifications of a bad land decision. However, most local real estate agencies will not have this knowledge.

Because new facilities, such as replacement hospitals, ambulatory surgery centers, cancer centers, and medical office buildings, are major investments, they must become an asset, not a liability, to the organization. Site selection is critical. The adequacy of a site for development depends on more than just cost and location. Form follows function; never allow the land to dictate the design of facilities. A site evaluation matrix (see the example on page 60) is useful in evaluating land options.

## Project Delivery Approach Selection

What project delivery approaches are available, and what are the pros and cons of each? Selection of a delivery approach is important and must be made early in the launch phase. The approach will drive the selection and formation of the project delivery team and development of the master project budget and schedule. The various delivery ap-

proaches will be discussed in more detail in Chapter 4.

## Project Delivery Team Organization

Is your internal team invested, educated, organized, and ready to begin? Do you have a structured and logical approach to external team member selection? The selection, formation, and functioning of the project delivery team is as critical to success as is the choice of delivery approach. The composition and roles of the internal and external project delivery teams will be discussed in more detail in Chapter 3.

## Alternative Financing Opportunities

With the 2008 collapse of the capital markets and the resulting reduction in equity values, the era of easy access to low-cost capital is certainly over for the foreseeable future. This has adversely affected the use of investment returns to fund capital projects. These events, combined with uncertain future reimbursement levels, have led healthcare owners implementing capital projects to explore alternative financing opportunities.

Such exploration should start early in the launch phase, as decisions made during this process could substantially affect the master project budget. Potential alternative financing opportunities include

- HUD Section 242 financing,
- third-party developers for non-acute care asset facilities,
- private–public partnerships for acute care asset facilities, and
- third-party development of central plant facilities.

## Integrated Process Planning

Form follows function—the 3F rule. It rolls easily off the tongues of healthcare planners and architects. So why is it so hard to apply? Traditionally, siloed user groups determine the space needs for a facility. This segregated decision making can lead to "form follows familiarity" instead of form follows function.

User groups generally meet weekly or monthly to discuss operations and room specifications for their departments. While it ensures user input and ultimately yields a room-by-room space listing, the isolated nature of this approach does not typically stimulate multidisciplinary process improvement discussions. Individual groups tend to design space around current departmental

processes rather than at a more appropriate cross-functional level.

The traditional, siloed model needs to change. Integrated process planning (illustrated in Exhibit 2.4), is a new paradigm in which a team is developed to tackle process flow, space programming, and schematic design at the same time. These processes are inextricably linked, and a team approach ensures that all parties are working toward a common goal.

It is imperative that the right resources are dedicated to space programming and design during the launch phase. Whether through Lean Processing, Six Sigma, or another approach, you should value-stream map the processes, get rid of the waste, and then program and design the facility based on the strategic scope and operational redesign. This requires participation from all who will use the new facility, including clinical, administrative, support, and ancillary services departments. The project delivery team must collaborate with and creatively challenge the users to design a program around needs and improved functions, not wants and outdated delivery models. Considering clinical and operational processes at an early stage will ensure that the facility design

**Exhibit 2.4: Integrated Process Planning**

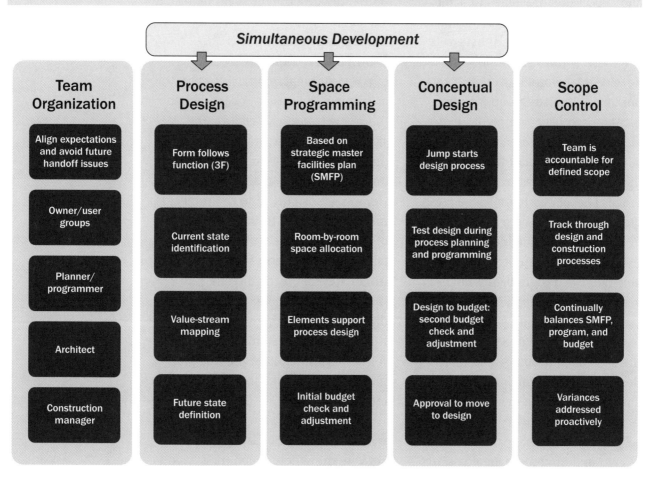

Simultaneous Development

| Team Organization | Process Design | Space Programming | Conceptual Design | Scope Control |
|---|---|---|---|---|
| Align expectations and avoid future handoff issues | Form follows function (3F) | Based on strategic master facilities plan (SMFP) | Jump starts design process | Team is accountable for defined scope |
| Owner/user groups | Current state identification | Room-by-room space allocation | Test design during process planning and programming | Track through design and construction processes |
| Planner/ programmer | Value-stream mapping | Elements support process design | Design to budget: second budget check and adjustment | Continually balances SMFP, program, and budget |
| Architect | Future state definition | Initial budget check and adjustment | Approval to move to design | Variances addressed proactively |
| Construction manager | | | | |

will enable growth, flexibility, and productivity. Operational and clinical issues to consider include the following:

- Patient access
- Wayfinding and entry points
- Utilization efficiencies
- Bed allocation and aggregation
- Care delivery models
- Adjacencies
- Supply chain management
- Utilization of tools and technology

Once the key processes are mapped and agreed upon, each user group will determine the ideal space and process relationships to achieve the ultimate patient, staff, and physician experience. The planners will use these "future state" flows to develop space programs that incorporate all the user groups' requirements. Each user group will then identify additional needs and desired adjacencies. It should take no more than three meetings to reach concurrence. The agreed-upon space program should then be tested against project budget guidelines.

Once the space program is developed, the design team will develop a conceptual plan to match process flows and programs. The team's next task will be to finalize the schematic design—the initial design phase in which the architect converts the listing of space to conceptual drawings. The process teams will be involved to ensure that value-stream and programmatic goals are met. Concurrently, other design team members will discuss infrastructure design to create the behind-the-walls elements of the design team's schematic product. This will be compared with the programs and process maps to avoid "scope creep." The involvement of the design team in the previous steps minimizes the risk of awkward handoffs and transla-

tion issues. At the conclusion of this phase, the design will again be tested against the budget to ensure that funding is adequate.

Scope creep, a major by-product of the traditional approach to programming and design, occurs when the scope is not managed by the same integrated team from start to finish. Controlling scope during the integrated process planning and design phases is critical to the project's financial success. In the early stages of the launch phase, the integrated team should develop a scope control model that feeds directly into the cost-control model. Exhibit 2.5 illustrates how scope should be controlled during the launch phase.

A typical integrated process planning phase will take four to six months.

## Master Project Budget

Do you know how much money you can spend on the project? Is your budget realistic, given the project scope? Do you know from what sources the money is coming? Answers to these questions are critical from day one.

Too often, CEOs and their chief financial officers (CFOs) wait until the design phase to develop the master project budget. Budgets developed

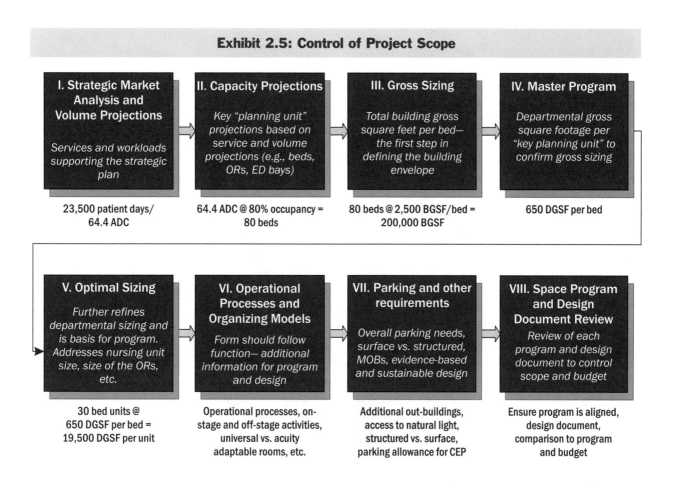

**Exhibit 2.5: Control of Project Scope**

**I. Strategic Market Analysis and Volume Projections**

*Services and workloads supporting the strategic plan*

23,500 patient days/ 64.4 ADC

**II. Capacity Projections**

*Key "planning unit" projections based on service and volume projections (e.g., beds, ORs, ED bays)*

64.4 ADC @ 80% occupancy = 80 beds

**III. Gross Sizing**

*Total building gross square feet per bed— the first step in defining the building envelope*

80 beds @ 2,500 BGSF/bed = 200,000 BGSF

**IV. Master Program**

*Departmental gross square footage per "key planning unit" to confirm gross sizing*

650 DGSF per bed

**V. Optimal Sizing**

*Further refines departmental sizing and is basis for program. Addresses nursing unit size, size of the ORs, etc.*

30 bed units @ 650 DGSF per bed = 19,500 DGSF per unit

**VI. Operational Processes and Organizing Models**

*Form should follow function— additional information for program and design*

Operational processes, on-stage and off-stage activities, universal vs. acuity adaptable rooms, etc.

**VII. Parking and other requirements**

*Overall parking needs, surface vs. structured, MOBs, evidence-based and sustainable design*

Additional out-buildings, access to natural light, structured vs. surface, parking allowance for CEP

**VIII. Space Program and Design Document Review**

*Review of each program and design document to control scope and budget*

Ensure program is aligned, design document, comparison to program and budget

at this point, however, often focus only on the construction cost. This is a critical mistake, because the total budget can be 1.5 to 1.7 times the construction cost. Exhibit 2.6 illustrates the major components and the percentage of the total budget each component uses. Expenditures for soft items, such as site evaluation and purchase, designers and consul-tants, medical equipment, medical technology, permits, and contingen-cies, are included in this total cost. It is essential to address all costs in the development of the budget. In addition, all expenditures should be tracked against the budget from day one so that all qualified expenses can be capitalized. Establishing the bud-get during the launch phase ensures

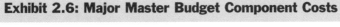

**Exhibit 2.6: Major Master Budget Component Costs**

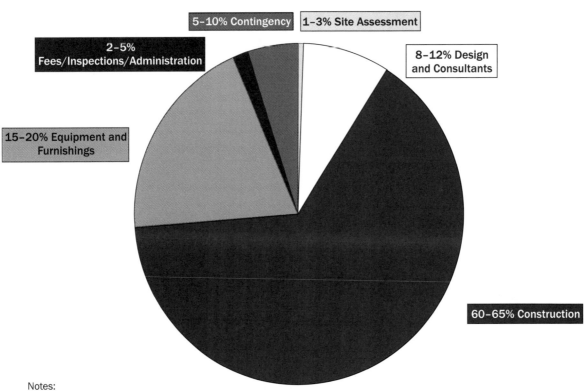

5–10% Contingency

1–3% Site Assessment

2–5% Fees/Inspections/Administration

8–12% Design and Consultants

15–20% Equipment and Furnishings

60–65% Construction

Notes:
1. Percentages vary depending on project location and scope.
2. No land costs or financing costs are assumed in the analysis.
3. Contingency assumes only owner contingency amount. Construction and other contingencies would be included in those components if required.

realistic financial goals and increases the likelihood that those goals will be met.

The master project budget is one of the first and most crucial project controls to put in place. If the project delivery team knows the master budget from the start, it can design a plan that fits that budget rather than design a budget that fits the plan.

The overall budget will be refined a number of times as you move from planning through programming and into the early design phase. You will eventually break down your costs into discrete project budget line items. This is an iterative process that may stop at a given point—such as during the board meeting that approves the project to proceed—or continue throughout the project. The scope of every aspect of the project becomes clearer over time. As you translate this information into defined cost estimates, you will be able to further refine each line item. However your organization ultimately decides to handle this, you should consider two important points.

First, it is difficult to anticipate all project needs early in the budget modeling phase. Contingency funds should be considered an essential part of your project budget. If you neglect to create a line item for these funds or skimp on them to make a budget look better, you place a significant risk on your project. The second point is that although construction accounts for a major portion of your budget, you still have other costs to consider. The budget should be broken down into the following major categories:

- **Site assessment costs:** Includes such items as surveying, environmental assessment, geotechnical evaluation, and the costs of the land.

- **Design and consultants:** Includes such items as design team fees, technology planner, medical equipment planner, and legal fees.
- **Construction:** Includes such items as temporary utilities, shell/core, building construction, special construction, and the costs of remediating the existing site.
- **Equipment and furnishings:** Includes such primary items as medical equipment, technology equipment/systems, foodservice, furniture/artwork, and signage/graphics/wayfinding.
- **Fees, testing, inspections, and administrative costs:** Includes such items as impact fees, materials testing, and training costs.
- **Financing costs:** Includes such items as interest expenses, costs for preparation of financing package, and overdraft fees.
- **Contingency:** Includes the cost to adequately manage the inherent risks on the project. Depending on the stage of the project, this amount should be between 5 and 10 percent of the total project budget.

A sample master project budget for a replacement hospital campus is included on page 64 to give the reader an idea of the level of detail required in such an undertaking. The example shows only the financial status summary sheets. However, the master budget includes other components, such as the budget detail reports (which show every cost change made to each budget line item within each major cost category) and the expense detail reports (which show every expenditure by budget line item).

In the end, budgeting success depends on three factors.

1. Know what you can afford, and make sure this target is communicated to the project delivery team early in the delivery process.
2. Start your cost modeling early, and update models often.
3. If costs exceed budget, refer back to number one.

## Master Project Schedule

Projects are complex and take time. What are your schedule goals and deadlines? Are these goals and deadlines realistic?

Perhaps no other document will be used more frequently throughout the course of a major project than the master project schedule. From the CEO to the field superintendent, the master schedule holds everyone accountable and ensures that all stakeholders know what is expected and when. Thorough input from every team member is paramount to making the master project schedule a useful and reliable tool.

Begin with the big picture in mind. One of the first tasks on any project is to determine the schedule. To make the schedule a reliable, functioning document, all team members must provide input on milestones and durations. The implementation expectations that result from such collaboration will be realistic and achievable.

As you begin developing the schedule, try to avoid getting bogged down in details. Remember, this is a working document that can be modified to include additional tasks later. By keeping the big picture in mind early in the process, the project delivery team can identify the major milestones and begin to develop the critical paths that will tie them together.

All key stakeholders must understand how the various components of the delivery process fit together and must abide by the timeline associated with each component. Like the master budget, the master schedule serves as a road map for the implementation of all phases, not just the construction phase. This schedule should track every step in every phase of the project, including the following:

- Regulatory agency approval process
- Integrated process planning
- Design
- Construction
- Financing
- Transition and occupancy

If developed properly and in a simple format (see the example on page 67), the schedule can be used not only to track progress and delays but also to rally support and build momentum for the project among the staff, board members, and the community.

## Medical Technology and Equipment Strategy

Equipment and technology are major components of the total project budget. The vision for the sophistication of equipment and technology will significantly affect the project cost.

Like the other steps in the launch gap analysis, this strategy cannot be developed in a silo. In fact, your master project budgeting effort must be based on the appropriate medical technology and equipment strategy. Because this line item can account

for up to 20 percent of your total budget, it demands early attention. Equally important, this strategy and the implementation of the medical technology and medical equipment plan will have lasting effects on your future operating capital commitments and operating model. This initial planning effort will have a strong effect on your ability to deliver your desired clinical outcome.

Developing your medical technology and equipment strategy should begin with the following objectives:

- **Develop an actionable road map.**
  - Create or confirm the foundation for your organization's medical technology and medical equipment.
  - Support information sharing and information management capabilities within the current facilities and in any new facility.
  - Ensure that the technology plan intersects appropriately with the facility/construction plan.
- **Confirm capital and operating cost models.**
  - Assist the organization in appropriately allocating funding with respect to facility-related capital, other capital, and operating dollars.

- Meet the current requirements and future needs.
- **Assess the organization's readiness to adopt new technologies.**
  - Capitalize on opportunities to improve efficiencies.
  - Identify potential barriers to acceptance.
  - Plan for implementation challenges.

While linked in a variety of ways, a medical equipment plan and a medical technology plan are different. Let's first look at each individually.

### WHAT IS MEDICAL EQUIPMENT PLANNING?

Medical equipment planning is the process of integrating the assessment, selection, and procurement of medical equipment into the overall project delivery process. Medical equipment has become more sophisticated, and health services providers rely on it to improve efficiency and patient throughput. However, equipment planning often becomes an afterthought in the design and construction process because owners (and teams) are focused on the bricks and mortar.

### WHAT IS TECHNOLOGY PLANNING?

Technology planning is the process of assessing current systems, identi-

fying technological needs, creating specifications and designs for major systems, and developing an accurate budget. Traditional technology consultants typically address the following system categories:

- Communications infrastructure
- Telephony
- Intercom
- Public address
- Security
- Television
- Wireless
- Video

Many organizations have begun to also address integration needs related to

- clinical systems, including electronic medical records, lab systems, radiology, clinical documentation, and dictation; and
- business systems, including patient accounting and registration, supply chains, and general ledger/HR/payroll.

### WHY IS EQUIPMENT AND TECHNOLOGY PLANNING SO IMPORTANT?

Medical equipment and technology affect the budget, schedule, and overall success of a capital project. Next to the building itself, they are the largest investments in a project.

The expertise of specialty consultants can guide you through crucial decisions in these areas. Without expert guidance, you may find yourself making costly corrections during construction or even after occupancy. Engaging a medical equipment planner and a medical technology planner in the project delivery process is key to a successful outcome. While many hospitals maintain extensive biomedical engineering, purchasing, and information technology departments, owners should consider involving outside consultants. On successful projects, the broader knowledge of outside subject matter experts frequently supports the knowledge and availability of internal team members.

With the advances in technology and equipment over the past ten years, it is easy to get distracted and confused. By planning early, engaging a multidisciplinary team, following a methodical process, and setting a realistic budget, you can ensure that the medical equipment and technology plan for your new facility will fulfill the expectations of your team and your patients.

## Regulatory Approval Process

Regulations, permits, inspections, licenses—the approval process can seem a bit daunting. When an organization decides to embark on a major project—be it replacement, reorganization, renovation, or expansion—it faces numerous requirements from regulatory bodies and jurisdictional authorities. Too often, external factors that may affect the scope and shape of the work are ignored as development moves forward. While these requirements cannot be circumvented entirely, they can be managed in tandem with project development. To coordinate the project with the various authorizations, appropriate consideration must be given to each individual requirement as soon as the project begins.

While it may seem like an obvious first step, the project definition determines the time frame and approvals necessary to begin construction. An understanding of the effect that regulatory approvals may have on the project schedule is essential. The current state of the economy has made financing and project approvals volatile. The baseline time frame will help the project advisor forecast a realistic cash flow, develop the completion schedule, and identify when to select key project team members.

Planning and management are critical at this phase. The project advisor should convene a "regulatory summit" to identify the laws and regulations governing the project. During the summit, the team should address individual roles and responsibilities, regulatory impact, scheduling, and compliance. The basic steps required for regulatory approval are as follows:

1. Obtain a certificate of need, if required.
2. Obtain drawings and specifications of your facility.
3. Plan approval by the department of health.
4. Perform construction progress inspections.
5. Perform the final construction inspection.
6. Obtain the required documentation at the final construction inspection.
7. Perform the licensing inspection.
8. Perform the certification inspection (if required).

## Transition and Occupancy Strategy

A move is a monumental event for staff, patients, families, and the community. The project delivery team has one chance to make a lasting impression with the transition and occupancy of a new facility, so planning for this phase should start early, during the launch gap analysis. In developing the strategy, the project team should consider the need to conduct a transition readiness assessment during the design phase, the need for outside assistance to help organize and implement the transition and occupancy plan, and the organization of the transition team. Exhibit 2.7 illustrates the key areas of focus that the transition and occupancy team should emphasize when developing the strategy for this phase.

The end work product of the project launch phase is a project implementation plan that includes the results of the gap analysis, a plan to fill the gaps, and a clear description of the project scope, budget, and schedule. This plan should be presented to the executive leadership team and the board for approval. Once approved, it becomes the road map for a successful project.

## KEY POINTS

Remember the following key points about the project launch phase:

- Define the Big Three: project scope, budget, and schedule.
- Complete a launch gap analysis.
- Develop the master project budget and schedule early, and share

**Exhibit 2.7: Major Transition and Occupancy Focus Areas**

them with key members of the project delivery team.

- Consider your desired future state when making land acquisition decisions.
- Implement integrated process planning prior to the design phase.

- Involve key members of the project delivery team at the beginning of the launch phase.
- Complete the launch phase with the development and approval of a comprehensive project implementation plan.

# CHAPTER 3

# The Project Delivery Team

## DO NOT OPERATE ALONE. THE ACTIVE, COLLABORATIVE, AND CONTINUOUS INVOLVEMENT OF KEY STAKEHOLDERS GREATLY AFFECTS SUCCESS.

At the onset of the launch phase, the CEO should select and organize the project delivery team. Just as a surgeon cannot operate alone, a CEO cannot embark on a major undertaking without help from people who have expertise in such projects. Exhibit 3.1 illustrates how internal and external specialists come together to form the project delivery team. As the exhibit shows, the team includes many key stakeholders.

The CEO leads the project through his or her role in the facilities planning committee (FPC), which is made up of internal and external project delivery team members. Active and continuous involvement of all members improves the potential for a successful outcome. This chapter describes the composition of the team and defines the roles and responsibilities of its members. ▶

**Exhibit 3.1: Project Delivery Team**

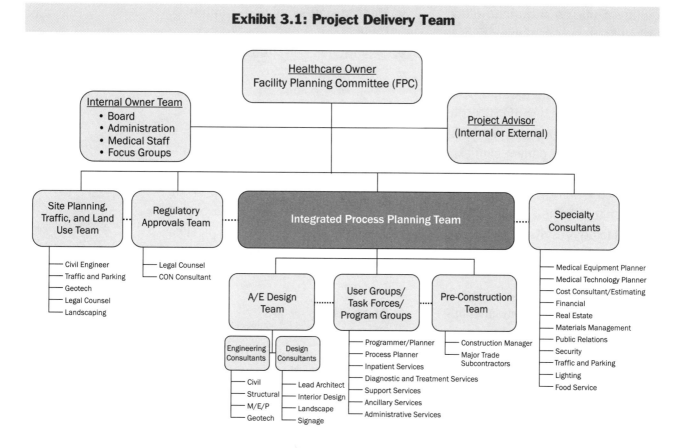

## THE INTERNAL TEAM: ORGANIZATION AND RESPONSIBILITIES

Before all else, form the internal team. This team is responsible for creating and realizing the project vision. It typically parallels the existing management and governance framework of the organization in that it involves the board, senior leaders, and medical staff. However, the internal team should also include individuals with experience in and knowledge of the specific needs and obligations of the project. The internal team typically controls internal and external resources. Internal leadership must maintain authority over and accountability for all team members.

The constitution of the internal team depends on the organization's culture. Some organizations allow only a select group of executives and senior-level staff to make key planning decisions. One stakeholder group that is often left out, however, is the medical staff. This is a critical mistake, because physicians bring clinical and patient care expertise to the equation. This expertise, combined with other stakeholders' capacity to plan and design a functional facility, results in a project that not only considers spatial needs but also addresses the medical component. Clinical or nursing leadership involvement is also often lacking. This is unfortunate as well, because these people bring patient advocacy and operational perspective to the process.

Regardless of who is selected to be on the team, the members need to know the team's purpose; the role, responsibility, and time commitment required of each member; and the effect of the team's work on the delivery process. The most successful projects are products of extensive involvement from the following stakeholders, each of which is discussed in the sections that follow:

- Facilities planning committee (FPC)
- Board of directors' building committee

- Medical staff's building committee (MSBC)
- Departmental task forces
- Focus groups

## Facilities Planning Committee

The FPC defines the project scope, makes key decisions, and keeps the project on track. The committee manages the day-to-day operations of the project and is ultimately responsible for its overall success. Typically, the FPC includes the following senior leaders:

- The CEO
- The chief operating officer
- A representative from the board of directors' building committee
- A representative of the medical staff's building committee
- The CFO
- The chief nursing officer
- The vice president of marketing and development
- The director of facilities
- A project advisor (this person may be from the internal or external team)

Including a member of the board's building committee and a member of the MSBC is important because these two stakeholder groups bring a different perspective to the team. The inclusion of these members on the FPC will increase buy-in and support for the project. Generally, the responsibilities of the FPC are as follows:

- Oversee the completion of a strategic master facilities plan.
- Establish the project's financial goals and objectives.
- Develop the project's vision, scope, and implementation plan.
- Make site-evaluation and land-purchase recommendations.
- Select the project delivery approach.
- Prequalify and select external members of the delivery team.
- Set and approve the project budget and schedule.
- Establish guiding design principles.
- Review and approve planning and design concepts.
- Oversee the approval of all contracts.

The FPC typically meets biweekly during the launch and design phases and monthly during subsequent phases.

## Board of Directors' Building Committee

As representatives of the local community, the board of directors "owns" the project. The board is usually involved in the delivery process through its building committee, which reports to the board on the progress of the project; a member of this committee should serve on the FPC. The building committee has two main responsibilities:

1. Oversee the entire delivery process.
2. Assist the CEO in publicizing and gaining community support for the project.

In addition, the committee gives final approval on the following:

- Land acquisition
- The project financial plan
- The project scope and implementation plan
- The design concept
- The construction contract

The board's building committee typically meets monthly to receive a project status report from the CEO and the FPC.

## Medical Staff's Building Committee

The MSBC coordinates the involvement of the medical staff in all phases of the delivery process. A member of the MSBC should be appointed to serve on the FPC to ensure that information flows from the FPC to the physicians and vice versa. The MSBC representative becomes the medical staff's project champion, communicating the physicians' input to the project delivery team.

The MSBC is made up of physicians from various medical staff groups, and it usually includes the following members:

- A chair (the project champion and usually the representative on the FPC)
- Three to four other physicians on the medical staff, one of whom is the chief of the medical staff
- A hospital administrator who is responsible for medical staff relations

Generally, the responsibilities of the MSBC are as follows:

- Assemble the medical staff user groups involved in departmental task forces.
- Monitor and coordinate the activities of the departmental task forces.
- Collect data and information from medical staff for consideration by the FPC.
- Disseminate information from the FPC to departmental task force

representatives and the entire medical staff.
- Ensure that the input of physicians and other clinical staff is considered throughout the delivery process.

The MSBC typically meets monthly. It gives an update on the project to the entire medical staff after each of these meetings.

## Departmental Task Forces

The departmental task forces play a pivotal role in the success of the project. They are the primary transmitters of user group information to the integrated process planning and design teams. Task force meetings are where the 3F theory (form follows function) comes into play. The primary focus of these groups is to ensure that the physical design supports efficient and effective care delivery processes. The physical and operational responses to departmental task forces' input are most commonly referred to as the functional program, or operational and space program (OSP).

The "space" portion of the OSP should not be totally driven by industry-standard space tables. Codes or standards of care drive much of the "space table" (e.g., scrub stations in the operating room, minimum room sizes, or medication areas on the nursing unit). Allowing each area of the facility to be programmed in a vacuum by user groups that do not represent the entire enterprise poses risks. For instance, how is it possible to accurately program and design the nursing unit for efficient delivery of medications without input from pharmaceutical and supply chain staff? Furthermore, shouldn't the method of medication delivery be consistent from unit to unit to achieve consistent clinical and operational performance? Interdepartmental, multidisciplinary task forces should initially program space before detailed design begins.

As Exhibit 3.2 shows, forming these task forces entails breaking up hospital functions and assigning each to a service category. Each category includes the following three major components of personnel involvement:

1. **Focus areas:** The primary functional areas of focus
2. **Process enablers:** The services that are critical to supporting the functions of the focus areas and that enable efficacious care and efficient patient throughput
3. **Impact groups:** Broad groups of personnel who have major day-to-day interactions with the focus areas and process enablers

A given department may be a focus area in one task force and a process enabler in another, as Exhibit 3.2 illustrates.

The size of these task forces varies depending on the services provided, with clinical areas requiring more members than administrative and support functions require. The time commitment for each member is approximately one to two days per month during the OSP and design stages of the delivery process. The departmental task forces are responsible for the following:

- Providing input on operational processes and space needs
- Reviewing and approving the space program and design concepts
- Participating in visits to other newly built or expanded facilities to verify the integrity of the project's operational and space concepts and design
- Analyzing mock-ups of various design ideas (for example, patient rooms, operating rooms, nursing stations) to test and confirm viability of the plan
- Participating in transition and occupancy planning

## Exhibit 3.2: Departmental Task Forces

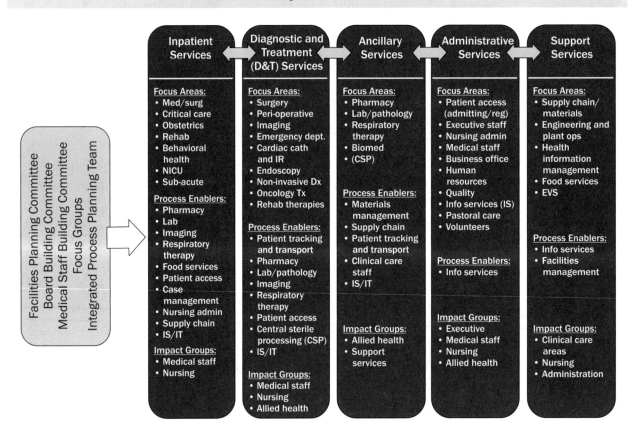

The task forces are part of the integrated process planning teams, and external members of these teams facilitate the task forces. These external members bring best practices to the task forces, test assumptions, begin to formulate physical solutions driven by the OSP, and help control scope to ensure an even balance with budget. The project advisor provides the necessary structure and controls while the teams ultimately report to the facility planning committee. Task forces meet monthly, in multiday sessions.

## Focus Groups

Focus groups offer valuable points of view to the delivery team. The group's feedback (positive and negative) and suggestions help the team provide a more patient- and family-oriented facility. In addition, focus groups can spread the word about the project and help gain community support.

During the strategic, project launch, and design phases, the team typically uses the following focus groups:

■ Patients (current and past)
■ Community leaders (city/county managers and/or commissioners)
■ Hospital staff (e.g., current and past nurses, maintenance workers)
■ Physicians

These focus groups are led by an outside facilitator or by the project advisor.

## Transition and Occupancy Planning Team

In the latter stages of design development, a transition and occupancy team should be established. This team (see Exhibit 3.3) will assist in clearly defining roles, responsibilities, and expectations for the transition and occupancy phase. The following steps should be performed to establish the teams and

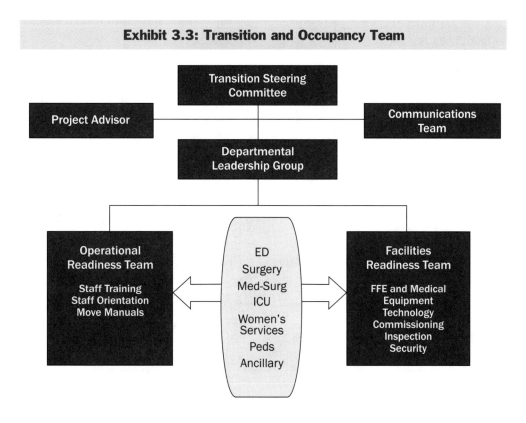

**Exhibit 3.3: Transition and Occupancy Team**

implement the transition and occupancy plan:

- Establish a transition steering committee and create an operational readiness assessment team, a facilities readiness assessment team, and additional task forces as needed.
- Ensure multidisciplinary participation, including representatives from front line clinical, support, ancillary, and administrative staff.
- Establish clear expectations and roles and responsibilities for each team.
- Set a meeting schedule and have clear agendas and objectives for each meeting.
- Involve external resources as needed (members of the project delivery team, such as the project advisor and technology and medical equipment specialists).
- Integrate external relocation specialists into the teams.

## THE EXTERNAL TEAM: ORGANIZATION AND RESPONSIBILITIES

No organization can embark on, let alone complete, a project without help from outside advisors who have knowledge of and experience in delivering an operationally efficient facility on time and within budget. The composition of the external team depends on the size and complexity of the project and the in-house capability of the organization, but the following roles should be filled in any undertaking:

- Project advisor
- Integrated process planning team
- Design team (i.e., an architect and engineering and design consultants)
- Construction manager
- Specialty consultants (e.g., legal, financial, food service, medical technology and equipment, independent cost)

The roles and responsibilities of each of these team members are discussed in the following sections.

### Project Advisor

Most major projects (generally those with a construction value greater than $10 million) need a project advisor—an individual or a firm that will oversee the entire delivery process—to ensure that the project runs smoothly and to intervene when needed.

Exhibit 3.4 illustrates the many tasks involved in a major project.

## Exhibit 3.4: What Must Be Managed During a Typical Project

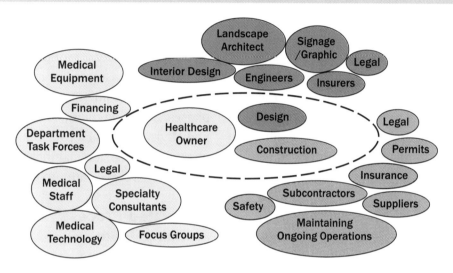

The project advisor is responsible for the day-to-day management of these myriad tasks. Therefore, the project advisor should have a comprehensive understanding of the multiple phases of the delivery process.

The major responsibilities of the project advisor are as follows:

- Complete, with the healthcare owner, a launch gap analysis.
- Organize and facilitate (assemble the members and coordinate the activities of) the FPC.
- Assist in site selection and land acquisition.

- Assist in the creation of the master project budget and schedule.
- Assist in the selection of the project delivery approach.
- Facilitate the selection and contract negotiation of all key external team members.
- Develop and maintain the project communications system.
- Create and maintain major-issues logs for the team.
- Coordinate the development of the project financial plan, the analysis of joint-venture opportunities, and the review of alternative funding sources.

- Oversee the regulatory review and approval process.
- Assist in developing a public relations and community support program.
- Manage the integrated process planning, design, and construction processes.
- Facilitate the project close-out, building commissioning, and occupancy of the facility.

The CEO has to decide whether the project advisor role should be filled internally or externally. This decision depends on the size and complexity of the project and whether any in-house team member has the necessary capability, experience, and time. Designating a project advisor before the launch phase ensures that the project has a leader early on. If the CEO is leaning toward using an internal advisor, he or she should consider hiring an external advisor to conduct the launch gap analysis. This will give the project process a strong start and keep it on course. As we previously stated, the end depends on the beginning. A capable external advisor will assist the FPC in selecting and forming the internal team, creating realistic budgets and schedules, making smart land-acquisition decisions, and negotiating construc-

tion contracts and hiring consultants. If the project is launched properly, subsequent phases will proceed smoothly. At this point, the organization can either continue using the outside advisor or use in-house personnel to handle the remaining phases. Selecting the most qualified advisor is crucial to the launch phase. This decision significantly affects the result of the project.

## Integrated Process Planning Team

In the early planning stages, bring together a planning team that will drive operational process review/redesign, programming, and conceptual design, all in an interrelated, coordinated effort. This approach avoids the handoffs and miscommunication often experienced with disassociated programmers and design teams and the scope and budget creep that can occur during the design phase. The planning team should include members with experience in operational process design/redesign, space programming, and conceptual design. Architectural firms may have internal personnel from all these disciplines, but in many cases, the team members come from several firms with expertise in each area.

The major responsibilities of this team are as follows:

- Assist in the organization and coordination of departmental task forces.
- Estimate and then verify patient volume and workload, which will drive space requirements.
- Value-stream map the current state of key operational processes to identify bottlenecks, external department connections, facility shortcomings, and points of customer interaction for each major hospital department.
- Value-stream map the future state for the highest volume patient types in each key specialty.
- Develop an owner's manual for operations at the new facility.
- Organize site visits to other hospitals to explore operational and design concepts that improve efficiency and cost.
- Develop space programs that outline the number, type, and size of rooms required for each department.
- Create conceptual (bubble) diagrams that illustrate the relationships and flows within and between each department.
- Guide the design team (architect and engineering and design

consultants) to ensure that approved guidelines for space allocation, operational relationships, and workflow are followed.

## Design Team

The design team typically consists of the following members:

- Architect (team leader)
- Engineering consultants
- Design consultants
- Construction manager

These professionals are important members of the delivery team and should be selected carefully. This selection should be based on qualifications, not price. In addition, because the internal team will be spending a tremendous amount of time with the design team, the chemistry or personality fit between these two groups should be taken into account.

For major projects, the engineering and design consultants should be under contract with the architect (who is under contract with the organization) so that coordination problems are minimized and the responsibility for the design is held by one entity. The design process involves tremendous coordination (for example, coordinating the civil and MEP drawings with the architectural drawings), and multiple design contracts only complicate the process further.

The roles and responsibilities of each design team member are discussed in the paragraphs that follow.

**ARCHITECT** The lead architect designs the overall structure of the project and establishes the design specifications the team will follow. The major responsibilities of the lead architect are as follows:

- Develop the master site plan.
- Work with the integrated process planning team to create the space program.
- Convert the operational and space programs to block diagrams.
- Create schematic design, design development, and construction documents.
- Help the delivery team (specifically, the construction manager) put together bid documents.
- Be involved in the bidding process and set the final construction price.
- Coordinate the acquisition of all required regulatory approvals and building permits.
- Oversee construction to ensure that the work complies with the approved construction documents and specifications.

- Review and approve required shop drawings during the construction phase.
- Review and make recommendations on requested change orders to the construction contract.
- Review and make recommendations on approval of the construction manager's application for payment.
- Ensure completion of punch lists and obtain substantial completion documentation.
- Provide final as-built documentation—that is, drawings that depict the actual work completed and put in place by the construction manager.

**ENGINEERING CONSULTANTS** The primary responsibilities of engineering consultants, who should be contracted by the lead architect, are to provide design support in their respective areas of expertise and assist the architect in ensuring that the facility is built in accordance with the design documents. These engineering consultants include

- civil engineers,
- structural engineers, and
- mechanical, electrical, and plumbing engineers.

**DESIGN CONSULTANTS** The work that design consultants provide is specialized and is not part of the basic services included in the standard American Institute of Architects' design contract. Therefore, design consultants must be hired separately. Major healthcare architecture firms have interior design, landscape architecture, and signage/graphic design capabilities, and the lead architect's firm may be able to provide these consultants, in which case these services can be added to the main architecture contract. But such services are also available through firms that specialize in this work. If the organization decides to use another firm for these services, it should ask the lead architect to coordinate the efforts of these designers. The following are design consultant specialties:

- Interior
- Landscape
- Signage and graphics
- Elevator
- Audiovisual

**CONSTRUCTION MANAGER** Because the construction phase is the riskiest, it must be managed appropriately. Therefore, the construction manager

(CM) is one of the most important members of the delivery team. The field of construction management came into existence in the 1980s, when many organizations downsized their in-house staffs and shifted the remaining responsibilities to outside companies. Because of the complexity of healthcare projects and their potential effects on continuing operations, the launch phase is the ideal time to bring the CM onto the team. Having a CM early in the process allows the team to develop detailed cost estimates as the design proceeds. This ensures that the project stays within the established budget and that the team understands the scope and costs before establishing the construction contract and starting the construction.

The CM and his or her team members must be selected based on their experience with similar healthcare projects. The primary responsibilities of the CM are as follows:

- Provide detailed construction budget estimates at each major stage of design—conceptual, schematic, design development, and construction.
- Provide detailed phasing options and construction schedules during the design phase.

- Provide constructability and alternative design options during the design phase.
- Manage the bidding process, which includes preparing instructions to bidders, prequalifying bidders, conducting pre-bid conferences, analyzing all bids, and making recommendations on awarding the subcontractor construction contracts.
- Develop the final construction costs.
- Oversee all construction activities.
- Ensure that the project is built in accordance with approved plans and specifications.
- Guarantee the quality of all work.
- Develop and maintain a job-site safety program.
- Establish and maintain the approved construction schedule.
- Obtain the certificate of occupancy.
- Close out all subcontractor contracts.

**SPECIALTY CONSULTANTS** Specialty consultants typically include, but are not limited to, the following professionals:

- **Attorneys or legal staff:** Review and approve contracts, give advice on land and zoning issues, develop all legal documents associated with financing, and assist with all regulatory review and approval issues
- **Financial planners:** Conduct a financial feasibility study, assess debt capacity, prepare a project financial plan, and help the bond sale
- **Real estate agents:** Assist in the purchase of land, lease medical office space, and help with zoning and land issues
- **Independent cost consultants:** Provide independent cost estimates at each budget update stage to compare and reconcile actual costs with the CM's estimates
- **Medical equipment planners:** Take inventory of existing medical equipment, plan necessary medical equipment, coordinate delivery and installation of medical equipment, prepare budget for medical equipment, and assist in developing the annual medical equipment budgets, as required
- **Medical technology planners:** Prepare necessary medical technology (low-voltage systems) equipment, coordinate delivery and installation of medical technology equipment, and prepare budget for medical technology

- **Food service planners:** In conjunction with the design team, design the food service component; create a list of new food service equipment to be purchased; coordinate the delivery and installation of food service equipment; and prepare budget for food service equipment
- **Materials management professionals:** In conjunction with the design team, design the materials management component and prepare budget for materials management
- **Public relations professionals:** Develop a public relations program to gain in-house and community support and develop and coordinate all major project events (e.g., groundbreaking, topping out, dedication)
- **Security planners:** In conjunction with the design team, design the security system and prepare the budget for it
- **Zoning professionals:** Assist in obtaining any necessary zoning amendments

## KEY POINTS

The following are key points to keep in mind during the selection and organization of the project delivery team:

- Organize the facilities planning committee first, and include board and medical staff members.
- Select external delivery team members (project advisor, lead architect, specialty consultants, and CM) during the launch phase.
- Identify champions of the project on the board, on the medical staff, and in the community, and involve them in the process.
- Select and involve departmental task forces in the integrated process planning and design. Ensure that these task forces keep an interdepartmental focus.
- Base selection of key external team members on qualifications, experience with similar projects, and chemistry with internal team members.

# CHAPTER 4

# Project Delivery Approaches

## CREATIVE CONTRACTING CAN GREATLY REDUCE PROJECT RISKS.

Any major project involves risk. Healthcare projects are especially risky, because they have the potential to disrupt life-saving services. During the project launch phase, the healthcare owner should select the delivery approach that best fits the project and minimizes risk.

A project delivery approach includes the planning, design, construction, and other services needed to organize, execute, and complete a project. Healthcare owners are exploring alternative approaches because the traditional approach (described in Exhibit 4.2) is outdated and inefficient, which makes it difficult to achieve desired outcomes. Despite decades of attempting to improve on traditional delivery approaches, projects are still over budget and delivered late. More important, the completed facilities often do not meet the basic goal of improving the operational efficiency of the organization. ▶

Understandably, owners are still searching for a reliable process with predictable outcomes. The industry is abuzz over new delivery approaches. The shift to a more integrated form of delivery has the greatest potential to improve on traditional approaches. Exhibit 4.1 illustrates the key trends driving the shift to integrated project delivery.

## WHAT IS INTEGRATED PROJECT DELIVERY?

Integrated project delivery (IPD) is a project delivery method distinguished by a contractual agreement among, at minimum, the owner, design professional, and builder where the risk and reward are shared and stakeholder success is dependent on project success. In

**Exhibit 4.1: Trends Driving Owners to IPD**

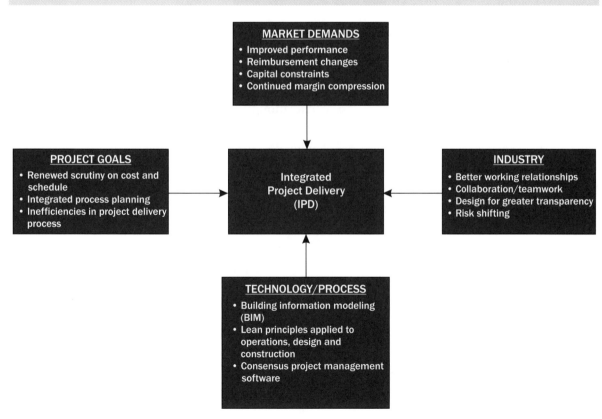

other words, true IPD is a collaborative capital-project delivery approach
that shares risk and reward via an
integrated agreement to reduce the
time and cost to bring a superior
product (new facility) to market.

IPD is relational, collaborative,
and Lean. It is *relational* because
the contract signed by all parties provides financial incentive to
mitigate risk. Its language prevents
pushing risk down the chain. IPD
is *collaborative* because it creates a
larger talent pool during the critical coordination stage of a project
and harnesses the insights of all
participants. The larger talent pool
comes from gathering all necessary expertise at the outset of the
project. Healthcare owners are
applying more Lean principles to
their operational processes. Trans-
ference of these same principles to
the capital delivery process should
be seamless. IPD applies the same
Lean principles to development and
thus reduces waste and optimizes
efficiency through all phases—design, fabrication, construction, and
occupancy. It creates an environment that allows proper allocation
of resources and responsibilities,
which reduces errors and avoids re-
work. Exhibit 4.2 compares the most
common traditional project delivery

approaches with IPD and lists the
pros and cons of each.

IPD is not the right approach for
every owner. The CEO and the project delivery team need to first understand and buy into the following
principles of IPD:

- Mutual respect and trust
- Mutual benefit and reward
- Collaborative innovation and
  decision making
- Early involvement of key partici-
  pants (design team, contractor,
  specialty consultants, and trade
  subcontractors)
- Early goal definition (scope,
  budget, and schedule)
- Integrated process planning
- Open communication
- Application of technology (e.g.,
  BIM)
- Application of Lean principles
  in planning, design, and
  construction

In addition, the healthcare owner
needs to fully understand how IPD
differs from traditional approaches in
the following critical areas:

- Teams
- Process
- Risk
- Compensation and reward

## Exhibit 4.2: Comparison of Project Delivery Approaches

| Delivery Approach | Characteristics | Pros | Cons |
|---|---|---|---|
| **Design Bid Award** | • Two main contracts (design team and contractor)<br>• Best understood<br>• Linear sequence of work (longest delivery) | • Low cost first | • Presents highest risk<br>• Stimulates adversarial relationships<br>• Encourages change orders<br>• Contractor has minimal input in design |
| **Design-Build** | • Single contract/responsibility<br>• Faster delivery<br>• Changes traditional roles and relationships between owner, contractor, and designer | • Sole source of accountability<br>• Increases potential for early completion<br>• Less adversarial<br>• Earlier knowledge of firm price | • Minimum innovative design potential<br>• Owner is less involved in design decisions<br>• Owner is pushed for earlier decisions<br>• Not "open book" on pricing and level of quality |
| **Construction Manager (CM-at-Risk)** | • Two main contracts (design team and contractor)<br>• Linear sequence of work but accommodates fast-track delivery<br>• CM is selected on qualifications, not price<br>• CM is selected early in delivery process | • Fosters more collaborative environment<br>• Allows for tight control of pricing and schedule<br>• Allows for phased construction<br>• Full disclosure of cost and schedule throughout delivery process<br>• Reduces owner risk | • Perception that price competition is limited<br>• Design team may not take input from CM during design<br>• Still can foster "finger pointing" behavior |
| **Integrated Project Delivery (IPD)** | • One integrated form of agreement<br>• Mutual respect and trust<br>• Mutual benefit and reward<br>• Early involvement of all key delivery team members<br>• Early goal definition | • Owner, architect, and contractor act as one<br>• Owner can tailor the best aspects of design-build and CM-at-risk<br>• Shared risk and rewards<br>• Allows for reduction of costs by eliminating redundant efforts<br>• Delivery relationships change from adversarial to collaborative<br>• Increases ability to deliver project within budget and schedule<br>• Increases ability to deliver a more operationally efficient facility | • Perception that cost competitiveness is limited<br>• Can be complex to administer<br>• Can require major culture change on part of owner, CM, and design team |

- Communication and technology
- Agreements

Exhibit 4.3 compares IPD and traditional project delivery in each of these areas. A final decision to go with IPD as the preferred delivery approach should only come after a thorough review of what makes IPD different and careful consideration of the answers to the following key questions:

1. Are the top leaders in your organization prepared to embrace and champion the principles of

## Exhibit 4.3: Traditional/Integrated Comparison

| Traditional Project Delivery | | Integrated Project Delivery |
| --- | --- | --- |
| Fragmented, assembled on an as needed or minimum-necessary basis, strongly hierarchical, controlled | Teams | An integrated team entity composed of key project stakeholders; assembled early in the process, open, collaborative |
| Linear, distinct, segregated; knowledge gathered as needed; information hoarded; silos of knowledge and expertise | Process | Concurrent and multilevel; early contributions of knowledge and expertise; information openly shared, stakeholder trust and respect |
| Individually managed, transferred to the greatest extent possible | Risk | Collectively managed, appropriately shared |
| Individually pursued, minimum effort for maximum return (usually zero first-cost based) | Compensation/ Reward | Team success tied to project success, value based |
| Paper based, two dimensional, analog | Communication/ Technology | Digitally based, virtual; building information modeling (three-, four-, and five-dimensional |
| Encourage unilateral effort, allocate and transfer risk, no sharing | Agreements | Encourage, foster, promote, and support multilateral open sharing and collaboration; risk sharing |

IPD? The support of the professionals involved in managing the day-to-day project activities is not enough.

2. Are you ready to move into trusting relationships with all team members within a short period of time? Trust is the cornerstone of IPD.

3. Is there a culture of continuous improvement in your organization? Willingness to innovate

and to improve tried-and-true processes must be present.

4. Is your organization prepared to take measured risks for the chance of more reward? The IPD agreement breaks away from the traditional protections of industry-standard contracts.

5. Are there individuals in your organization who could impede an IPD process? Leaders must be prepared to remove any

individual who could derail the IPD process.

6. Is your organization considering IPD as a competitive advantage because of the buzz or because it is committed to improving the performance of the industry? The success of an IPD project depends on the commitment and understanding of all team members.

7. Is your organization completely focused on the bottom line? The IPD process seeks to harness individual talent from the project's inception, sometimes at a higher initial cost than traditional contracting methods require. Neither a low-bid mentality nor padded fees to protect against the unknowns of a new process are part of IPD.

8. Does your organization have the patience to trust the process and allow it to work? The journey into IPD is new for many participants. They must be patient as traditional barriers are broken down and organizations enter uncharted waters together.

9. Is your organization fragmented and not internally collaborative? Collaboration starts from within. The spirit must be present in your organization before it can be evident in your relationships with other project team members.

10. Does your organization fully understand IPD and the ideals that surround it? Each organization must be thoroughly educated on what makes IPD successful to evaluate whether it aligns with the organization's culture and values.

The successful IPD project is the product of a network of individuals who are thirsty for knowledge, egoless, reflective, responsive, inquisitive, solution driven, and compelled to serve a mission greater than those of their own firms. Decisions are based on the good of the project, sometimes at the expense of a team member's own organization. As we discussed, the process for evaluating whether IPD is right for the proposed project and whether the organization is qualified to implement IPD is very specific. Exhibit 4.4 can serve as a guide to take the owner through this decision making process.

The two most important factors in making IPD a success are team selection and the development of an integrated form of agreement (IFOA).

## Exhibit 4.4: IPD Team Selection Process

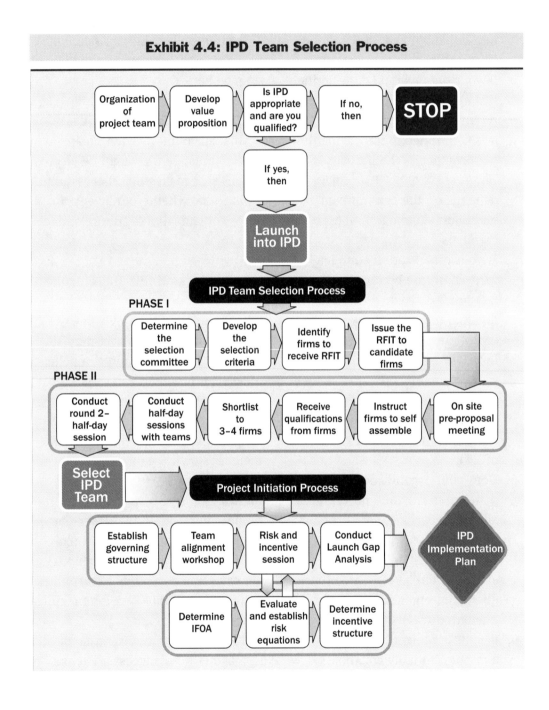

## Team Selection

Once you have thoroughly evaluated your organization, have developed a value proposition, and are committed to IPD, it is time to select your team. It is important to witness interactions among potential team members and the organization staff to evaluate their chemistry. The easiest way to accomplish this is to conduct a series of planned interactions. Selection is more art than science in an IPD project, as you evaluate the team member's ability to be relational, collaborative, and Lean. These are not exactly quantitative elements. Exhibit 4.4 highlights the recommended team selection process under IPD. Each step in the process is explained in detail in the sections that follow.

### Step 1: Determine the Selection
Committee    The committee should be a mix of top organizational leaders and project stakeholders. Members should be prepared to invest quite a bit of time into the selection process and should not miss any interactions with potential teams.

### Step 2: Develop the Team Selection
Criteria    In this step, IPD truly differentiates itself from traditional delivery methods. As stated previously, IPD team selection is an art. It is based more on behavior than on qualification and fee. While hiring a qualified team that has experience delivering your type of project is still important, it is more important to select individuals with the aptitude and enthusiasm for delivering integrated services.

### Step 3: Identify Potential Firms    This is where you, the owner, can include any and all firms of which you have prior knowledge or with which you have a previous relationship. To ensure that you select the best possible team to complete the task, you must be honest with yourself and eliminate those firms that would be chosen solely for political purposes. In IPD, all roads lead back to the self-evaluation process. If you are not truly ready, do not begin the journey.

Make a list of possible architects and construction managers with the skills and qualifications necessary for the scope of the project. Include engineers or prime specialty consultants, such as medical equipment and technology planners. Once the list is complete, create a request for integrated team (RFIT) that outlines the process and criteria for selection.

**Step 4: Issue the RFIT** Once the RFIT has been distributed and each company has responded, the following process should be implemented:

- Plan an initial site visit with each firm on your list.
- Request self-assembly of a team based on cross relationships among firms listed in the RFIT.
- Review each integrated team's submittal of qualifications based on instructions in the RFIT.
- Short-list three to four teams that will continue the process.
- Conduct a half-day workshop with each short-listed team.
- Conduct a final half-day presentation for each remaining team. (There should be no more than two teams at this point.)

**Step 5: Select the IPD Team** The selection committee should now review its selection criteria and meet one week after final presentations. This gives each committee member time to fully analyze the interactions throughout the entire process. Because each team visit was followed by a committee assessment and recap, documentation of thoughts and concerns should be sufficient to thoroughly evaluate each group. Each committee member should complete a final evaluation form for each team and then vote for his or her final choice. To keep it simple, the team with the most votes wins. If the vote ends in a tie, the committee should consider an additional team interaction.

IPD team selection requires a significant time investment from the selection committee and the teams. The entire process, from the formation of the selection committee to the final decision, can take 60 to 120 days. Because the short-listed teams invest so much time, consideration for reimbursement is appropriate. The work product of each team, regardless of whether it was selected, will add value to the project. The offer of reimbursement strongly demonstrates the owners' commitment to developing a truly integrated team.

## Selecting the Appropriate IPD Agreement

The owner's readiness to enter into an IPD arrangement drives the contracting process. Representatives from legal and risk management should be involved in document selection. After a review of all the available agreements, industry experts say that the ConsensusDOCS 300 is a better place to start than the American Institute of Architects family of documents. Overall, the ConsensusDOCS 300 appear to better promote collaboration and align the interests of the owner, architect, and contractor in terms of sharing risks and rewards. The ConsensusDOCS 300 includes the following features:

- The overall purpose of the ConsensusDOCS 300 is to form a collaborative team that is focused on maximizing quality while controlling price and schedule.
- The contract's self-proclaimed objective is "to design and construct the facilities called for in the Owner's Program, within the Project Target Cost Estimate and the Schedule developed under the Agreement."
- The agreement's goal is to align the interests of the owner, architect, and contractor so that all parties share risks and rewards.
- The agreement adequately and equitably addresses the owner's "hot-button issues."
- The contract adopts principles of collaboration and Lean project delivery.

- This approach recognizes that each party's success is tied directly to the success of all other members of the collaborative project team and encourages and requires the parties to organize and integrate their respective roles, responsibilities, and expertise; to identify and align their respective expectations and objectives; to commit to open communications, transparent decision making, proactive and non-adversarial interaction, problem solving, and the sharing of ideas; to continuously seek to improve the project planning, design, and construction processes; and to share both the risks and rewards associated with achieving the project objectives.
- The ConsensusDOCS contract agreement does not create a single-purpose entity, making the use of this document less complicated.

In summary, the critical success factors for an IPD project are

- a knowledgeable and committed owner,
- an effective charter established early on to delineate clear lines of communication,

- a core experienced project team built on trust, and
- a contract that rewards all parties for teamwork.

If a capital expansion project is the solution to a critical need, consider using an integrated and collaborative approach to delivering the project. IPD can generate efficiencies in time and budget by bringing owners, contractors, consultants, architects, and vendors onto the same team under a single set of contract, risk, and reward agreements. This creates focus and rewards each team member for achieving optimal project results.

Evaluation of whether the IPD process is right for a particular owner and project should happen in the earliest project discussions. Trust in and by all parties who will contribute to delivery determines the success of an IPD approach.

## KEY POINTS

Remember the following points about minimizing risk through creative project delivery approaches:

- The selection of a project delivery approach is the riskiest decision for the organization during the delivery process because it has the greatest effect on cost and schedule.
- The best approach to your project is the one that has the best chance of creating a collaborative team environment, because such an environment encourages success.
- Integrated project delivery is the approach with the greatest chance of ensuring project success.

# Conclusion

I hope this book has emphasized the importance of a structured project delivery process and the valuable contribution of the launch phase. The time invested in the launch phase yields a multitude of benefits. At minimum, it ensures the timely and cost-efficient delivery of a facility, and at maximum, it enhances daily operations and ensures customer satisfaction.

I have intended this book to serve as a roadmap for launching a project. The key points in each chapter serve as landmarks by which you can denote your progress along the way. Please consult those landmarks as you go.

The key takeaways are as follows:

- Conduct a launch gap analysis as the first step in implementing a capital project.
- Implement integrated process planning early in the design phase.
- Consider integrated project delivery as the preferred project delivery approach.

In summary, keep these messages in mind. First, stick patiently to the process, and do not jump into the next step until the last one is completed. Second, you cannot do this alone, so engage the help of experts. Lastly, keep your sense of humor and make the project not just professionally rewarding but personally fulfilling for you and all the participants.

# Suggested Reading

American Hospital Association and American College of Healthcare Executives. 2009. *Futurescan 2009*. Chicago: Society for Healthcare Strategy and Market Development and Health Administration Press.

Black, J., and D. Miller. 2008. *The Toyota Way to Healthcare Excellence: Increase Efficiency and Improve Quality with Lean*. Chicago: Health Administration Press.

Goldman, E. F. 2002. *Results-Oriented Strategic Planning*. Chicago: Society for Healthcare Strategy and Market Development.

Hayward, C. 2005. *Healthcare Facility Planning: Thinking Strategically*. Chicago: Health Administration Press.

KLMK Group, LLC. 2010. "Integrated Project Delivery: The Value Proposition—An Owners Guide for Launching a Healthcare Capital Project via IPD." White paper. Richmond, VA: KLMK Group, LLC.

Luke, R. D., PhD; S. L. Walston, PhD; and P. M. Plummer. 2003. *Healthcare Strategy: In Pursuit of Competitive Advantage*. Chicago: Health Administration Press.

Malkin, J. 2008. *A Visual Reference for Evidence-Based Design*. Concord, MA: Center for Health Design.

Marberry, S. O. 2006. *Improving Healthcare with Better Building Design*. Chicago: Health Administration Press.

Rice University Building Institute. 2007. *The Latest Thinking: Project Delivery Strategies for Healthcare Buildings*. Houston, TX: Rice University Building Institute.

Smith, A. C., R. Barry, and C. E. Brubaker. 2007. *Going Lean: Busting Barriers to Patient Flow*. Chicago: Health Administration Press.

Sussman, J. H. 2007. *The Healthcare Executive's Guide to Allocating Capital*. Chicago: Health Administration Press.

Zuckerman, A. J. 2005. *Healthcare Strategic Planning*, 2nd edition. Chicago: Health Administration Press.

# KLMK
*group*

## Site Evaluation Matrix

Rate the following issues. In the first column of each site location, write a score:

1 (Excellent)....................5 (Poor)

| | Site 1 Location | Site 2 Location |
|---|---|---|
| **I. FINANCIAL CRITERIA**<br>These factors affect the total actual cost of the site. | | |
| **A. Acquisition Costs**<br>*The purchase price of the property and other costs related to controlling the site.* | | |
| 1. *Purchase Price*<br>Price per acre, total acreage, and total cost. | | |
| 2. *Control Costs*<br>The cost of options or other measures required to gain control of the site. | | |
| **B. Preparation Costs**<br>These figures help examine costs which differentiate one site from another, not those costs which would be incurred on any site. | | |
| 1. *Cost of Grading*<br>The cost of shaping the site for typical hospital use (i.e., a hilly site would cost more to prepare than a relatively flat one). | | |
| 2. *Cost for Water*<br>The cost (if any) to run water lines with adequate capacity to the site. | | |
| 3. *Cost for Sewer*<br>The cost (if any) to run sanitary and storm sewer lines to the site. This should include any costs of required additional construction, such as pumping stations, major drainage structures, etc. | | |

KLMK Group, LLC 2002

Page 1 of 4

Site Selection Matrix
1/29/10

# KLMK
*group*

## Site Evaluation Matrix

Rate the following issues. In the first column of each site location, write a score:

*1 (Excellent)..................5 (Poor)*

| | Site 1 Location | Site 2 Location |
|---|---|---|
| **4. *Cost for Power/Phone*** <br> The cost of bringing power and phone service (including fiber optics for computer labs) to the site. | | |
| **5. *Cost for Gas*** <br> The cost of bringing gas service to the site. | | |
| **6. *Cost for Road Improvements*** <br> The cost of building and/or upgrading roads to bring traffic to the site. This may include widening, traffic signals, and other improvements. | | |
| **7. *Cost to Rezone & Adjust Easements*** <br> Expected costs (legal, etc.) to rezone property, if required, or to obtain conditional use permits, variances, etc. | | |
| **8. *Additional Site Costs*** <br> Are there any other potential extra costs related to the site? Have preliminary geotechnical and environmental (Phase I) studies been performed? | | |
| **Scoring Total:** | | |
| *Summary* | | |
| *Summary of Non-Financial Criteria* | | |

Site Selection Matrix
1/29/10

# Site Evaluation Matrix

Rate the following issues. In the first column of each site location, write a score:

1 (Excellent)...................5 (Poor)

| | Site 1 Location | Site 2 Location |
|---|---|---|
| **II. NON-FINANCIAL CRITERIA** | | |
| **A. Access Issues** | | |
| *The importance of these factors is determined largely by the sensitivity of your planned patient population to the hospital's location. If the location (convenience, travel time, etc.) could affect the patients' choices of whether to go there, these factors will be very important.* | | |
| 1. *Access from Service Areas (Strategically Appropriate)* Is the site located near, or within, a large portion of the pool of potential patients? | | |
| 2. *Access and Visibility from Major Roads* Is the site within a short distance from major travel arteries? | | |
| 3. *Traffic Impacts* To what degree will traffic patterns be changed? | | |
| 4. *Ease of Road Access* Is the road network immediately around the site sufficient to handle the traffic generated by the hospital? | | |
| **B. Site Issues** | | |
| *These factors evaluate, in a qualitative sense, the site and its surroundings.* | | |
| 1. *Compatibility of Existing Land Uses* Are the current surroundings compatible with hospital use, based on noise, traffic, or other issues? | | |
| 2. *Compatibility of Planned Land Uses* Even if the surrounding land is not yet developed, will the planned uses be compatible? Considering the strength of any developers involved, how likely is it that planned development will be executed? | | |
| 3. *Site Configuration* Is the site shaped to allow maximum flexibility (i.e., square, rectangular) and not irregular? | | |

KLMK Group, LLC 2002

Site Selection Matrix
1/29/10

**KLMK** _group_

## Site Evaluation Matrix

Rate the following issues. In the first column of each site location, write a score:

1 (Excellent)..................5 (Poor)

| | Site 1 Location | | Site 2 Location | |
|---|---|---|---|---|
| 4. *Geological Concerns* <br> Will the geology drive expensive foundation costs? | | | | |
| 5. *Environmental Issues* <br> Are there potential environmental Issues that will drive costs of site preparation? | | | | |
| 6. *Site Configuration* <br> Is the site shaped to allow maximum flexibility (i.e., square, rectangular) and not irregular? | | | | |
| 7. *Space for Future Expansion* <br> Is the site large enough to allow expansion of the facility to accommodate more patients? Is there room to develop future support functions? | | | | |
| 8. *Site Views* <br> Do the surrounding properties and other features provide good views from the site (especially forest or open spaces)? | | | | |
| **Scoring Total:** | | | | |
| *Summary* <br><br> *Summary of Non-Financial Criteria* | | | | |

Site Selection Matrix
1/29/10

# KLMK group

## SAMPLE MASTER PROJECT BUDGET SUMMARY REPORT — COMMITTED + EXPENDED

November 28, 2009

| PROJECT: 1000.1 | NEW HOSPITAL PROJECT | | | | | MANAGER : DUKE |
|---|---|---|---|---|---|---|
| BUDGET ITEM | CURRENT BUDGET | COMMITTED TO DATE | BALANCE TO COMMIT | EXPENDED TO DATE | BALANCE TO COMPLETE | % COMPLETE |
| **1000 - SITE ACQUISITION** | | | | | | |
| 1101  SITE – MASTER SITE PLANNING | $ 35,000 | $ 0 | $ 35,000 | $ 0 | $ 35,000 | 0.0% |
| 1205  SITE – GEOTECHNICAL INVESTIGATION | $ 32,700 | $ 32,700 | $ 0 | $ 32,277 | $ 423 | 98.7% |
| SUBTOTAL 1000 SITE ACQUISITION | $ 67,700 | $ 32,700 | $ 35,000 | $ 32,277 | $ 35,423 | |
| **2000 - DESIGN / CONSULTANTS** | | | | | | |
| 2101  DES – FEASIBILITY STUDY | $ 380,000 | $ 380,000 | $ 0 | $ 380,000 | $ 0 | 100.0% |
| 2102  DES – FEASIBLITY STUDY REIMBURSABLES | $ 98,992 | $ 98,992 | $ 0 | $ 98,992 | $ 0 | 100.0% |
| 2105  DES – STRATEGIC PLANNING | $ 63,050 | $ 63,049 | $ 1 | $ 63,049 | $ 1 | 100.0% |
| 2106  DES – STRATEGIC PLANNING REIMBURSABLES | $ 19,982 | $ 19,982 | ($ 0) | $ 19,982 | ($ 0) | 100.0% |
| 2109  DES – FUNCTIONAL PROGRAMMING | $ 375,435 | $ 375,435 | $ 0 | $ 233,050 | $ 142,385 | 62.1% |
| 2110  DES – FUNCTIONAL PROGRAMMING REIMBURSABLES | $ 75,000 | $ 42,361 | $ 32,639 | $ 42,361 | $ 32,639 | 56.5% |
| 2115  DES – TRAFFIC ENGINEER | $ 55,000 | $ 45,900 | $ 9,100 | $ 49,571 | $ 5,429 | 90.1% |
| 2201  DES – ARCHITECTURE & ENGINEERING FEE | $ 10,987,826 | $ 10,358,700 | $ 629,126 | $ 173,038 | $ 10,814,788 | 1.6% |
| 2202  DES – A & E REIMBURSABLES | $ 700,018 | $ 708,867 | ($ 8,849) | $ 8,849 | $ 691,169 | 1.3% |
| 2204  DES – CIVIL ENGINEERING FEE | $ 900,000 | $ 171,574 | $ 728,427 | $ 175,716 | $ 724,284 | 19.5% |
| 2205  DES – CIVIL ENGINEERING REIMBURSABLES | $ 13,000 | $ 3,508 | $ 9,492 | $ 3,508 | $ 9,492 | 27.0% |
| 2208  DES – MEP ENGINEERING FEES | $ 5,406,414 | $ 4,410,000 | $ 996,414 | $ 398,950 | $ 5,007,464 | 7.4% |
| 2209  DES – MEP ENGINEERING REIMBURSABLES | $ 270,000 | $ 16,284 | $ 253,716 | $ 16,284 | $ 253,716 | 6.0% |
| 2301  DES – LANDSCAPE ARCHITECTURE FEE | $ 135,000 | $ 0 | $ 135,000 | $ 0 | $ 135,000 | 0.0% |
| 2303  DES – INTERIOR DESIGN FEE | $ 365,000 | $ 0 | $ 365,000 | $ 0 | $ 365,000 | 0.0% |
| 2305  DES – SIGNAGE/GRAPHICS DESIGN FEE | $ 140,000 | $ 0 | $ 140,000 | $ 0 | $ 140,000 | 0.0% |
| 2310  DES – MEDICAL EQUIPMENT PLANNING | $ 790,000 | $ 790,000 | $ 0 | $ 24,000 | $ 766,000 | 3.0% |
| 2311  DES – MEDICAL EQUIP PLANNING REIMBURSABLES | $ 84,000 | $ 3,984 | $ 80,016 | $ 3,984 | $ 80,016 | 4.7% |
| 2315  DES – TECHNOLOGY CONSULTING FEE | $ 88,000 | $ 88,000 | $ 0 | $ 0 | $ 88,000 | 0.0% |
| 2316  DES – TECHNOLOGY CONSULTING REIMB. | $ 17,600 | $ 0 | $ 17,600 | $ 0 | $ 17,600 | 0.0% |
| 2320  DES – FOOD SERVICE CONSULTING FEE | $ 57,000 | $ 0 | $ 57,000 | $ 0 | $ 57,000 | 0.0% |
| 2403  DES – PRECONSTRUCTION SERVICES | $ 800,000 | $ 800,000 | $ 0 | $ 424,946 | $ 375,054 | 53.1% |
| 2404  DES – PROGRAM MANAGEMENT | $ 2,900,000 | $ 2,900,000 | $ 0 | $ 260,000 | $ 2,640,000 | 9.0% |
| 2405  DES – PROGRAM MANAGEMENT REIMBURSABLES | $ 960,000 | $ 52,267 | $ 907,733 | $ 52,267 | $ 907,733 | 5.4% |

page 1

64 | SAMPLE MASTER PROJECT BUDGET

# KLMK group

## SAMPLE MASTER PROJECT BUDGET SUMMARY REPORT — COMMITTED + EXPENDED

November 28, 2009

**PROJECT: 1000.1**  NEW HOSPITAL PROJECT

**MANAGER : DUKE**

| BUDGET ITEM | CURRENT BUDGET | COMMITTED TO DATE | BALANCE TO COMMIT | EXPENDED TO DATE | BALANCE TO COMPLETE | % COMPLETE |
|---|---|---|---|---|---|---|
| 2406  DES – MATERIALS MANAGEMENT CONSULTANT | $ 128,000 | $ 116,000 | $ 12,000 | $ 73,375 | $ 54,625 | 57.3% |
| 2407  DES – LEGAL FEES | $ 250,000 | $ 18,203 | $ 231,797 | $ 18,203 | $ 231,797 | 7.3% |
| 2412  DES – MATERIALS MANAGEMENT REIMBURSABLES | $ 2,500 | $ 2,266 | $ 234 | $ 2,266 | $ 234 | 90.6% |
| 2513  DES – GEOTECHNICAL ENGINEERING FEES | $ 44,100 | $ 44,100 | $ 0 | $ 44,100 | $ 0 | 100.0% |
| SUBTOTAL 2000 DESIGN / CONSULTANTS | $ 26,105,917 | $ 21,509,471 | $ 4,596,446 | $ 2,566,491 | $ 23,539,426 | |
| **3000 - CONSTRUCTION** | | | | | | |
| 3401  CONST – CM GUARANTEED MAXIMUM PRICE | $ 245,277,640 | $ 0 | $ 245,277,640 | $ 0 | $ 245,277,640 | 0.0% |
| SUBTOTAL 3000 CONSTRUCTION | $ 245,277,640 | $ 0 | $ 245,277,640 | $ 0 | $ 245,277,640 | |
| **4000 - EQUIPMENT / FURNITURE** | | | | | | |
| 4100  EQUIP – MEDICAL EQUIPMENT | $ 35,000,000 | $ 0 | $ 35,000,000 | $ 0 | $ 35,000,000 | 0.0% |
| 4200  EQUIP – TECHNOLOGY EQUIPMENT | $ 15,000,000 | $ 0 | $ 15,000,000 | $ 0 | $ 15,000,000 | 0.0% |
| 4301  EQUIP – KITCHEN EQUIPMENT | $ 2,600,000 | $ 0 | $ 2,600,000 | $ 0 | $ 2,600,000 | 0.0% |
| 4401  EQUIP – FURNITURE/FURNISHINGS | $ 5,850,000 | $ 0 | $ 5,850,000 | $ 0 | $ 5,850,000 | 0.0% |
| 4403  EQUIP – ARTWORK | $ 150,000 | $ 0 | $ 150,000 | $ 0 | $ 150,000 | 0.0% |
| 4404  EQUIP – GRAPHICS/SIGNAGE | $ 900,000 | $ 0 | $ 900,000 | $ 0 | $ 900,000 | 0.0% |
| SUBTOTAL 4000 EQUIPMENT / FURNITURE | $ 59,500,000 | $ 0 | $ 59,500,000 | $ 0 | $ 59,500,000 | |
| **5000 - FEES / INSPECT / ADMIN** | | | | | | |
| 5101  FEES – CITY FEES | $ 3,800 | $ 1,870 | $ 1,930 | $ 1,870 | $ 1,930 | 49.2% |
| 5103  FEES – STATE FEES | $ 115,000 | $ 0 | $ 115,000 | $ 0 | $ 115,000 | 0.0% |
| 5104  FEES – BUILDING PERMIT FEES | $ 210,000 | $ 0 | $ 210,000 | $ 0 | $ 210,000 | 0.0% |
| 5108  FEES – EPA FEES | $ 10,300 | $ 0 | $ 10,300 | $ 0 | $ 10,300 | 0.0% |
| 5109  FEES – SEWER TAP FEE | $ 1,172,300 | $ 0 | $ 1,172,300 | $ 0 | $ 1,172,300 | 0.0% |
| 5111  FEES – UTILITY CONNECTION FEES | $ 1,300 | $ 0 | $ 1,300 | $ 0 | $ 1,300 | 0.0% |
| 5302  FEES – MATERIALS TESTING | $ 925,000 | $ 0 | $ 925,000 | $ 0 | $ 925,000 | 0.0% |
| 5307  FEES – PHYSICIST TESTING | $ 7,500 | $ 0 | $ 7,500 | $ 0 | $ 7,500 | 0.0% |
| 5310  FEES – COMMISSIONING AGENT FEES | $ 1,202,203 | $ 0 | $ 1,202,203 | $ 0 | $ 1,202,203 | 0.0% |
| 5403  FEES – MISCELLANEOUS ADMINISTRATIVE EXPENSES | $ 250,000 | $ 0 | $ 250,000 | $ 0 | $ 250,000 | 0.0% |

Project Link Software

page 2

**KLMK** group

## SAMPLE MASTER PROJECT BUDGET SUMMARY REPORT — COMMITTED + EXPENDED

November 28, 2009

**PROJECT: 1000.1**     NEW HOSPITAL PROJECT

**MANAGER : DUKE**

| BUDGET ITEM | CURRENT BUDGET | COMMITTED TO DATE | BALANCE TO COMMIT | EXPENDED TO DATE | BALANCE TO COMPLETE | % COMPLETE |
|---|---|---|---|---|---|---|
| 5500 FEES – OCCUPANCY AND RELOCATION | $ 1,500,000 | $ 0 | $ 1,500,000 | $ 0 | $ 1,500,000 | 0.0% |
| 5501 FEES – BUILDER'S RISK INSURANCE | $ 600,000 | $ 0 | $ 600,000 | $ 0 | $ 600,000 | 0.0% |
| 5502 FEES – WRAP-UP INSURANCE | $ 3,701,731 | $ 0 | $ 3,701,731 | $ 0 | $ 3,701,731 | 0.0% |
| 5507 FEES – UMBRELLA INSURANCE | $ 1,222,700 | $ 0 | $ 1,222,700 | $ 0 | $ 1,222,700 | 0.0% |
| SUBTOTAL 5000 FEES / INSPECT / ADMIN | $ 10,921,834 | $ 1,870 | $ 10,919,964 | $ 1,870 | $ 10,919,964 | |
| **7000 - CONTINGENCY** | | | | | | |
| 7307 CTGCY – IPD TEAM CONTINGENCY | $ 22,785,676 | $ 0 | $ 22,785,676 | $ 0 | $ 22,785,676 | 0.0% |
| 7501 CTGCY – WRAP-UP CONTINGENCY | $ 2,341,233 | $ 0 | $ 2,341,233 | $ 0 | $ 2,341,233 | 0.0% |
| 7700 CTGCY – OWNER CONTINGENCY | $ 18,000,000 | $ 0 | $ 18,000,000 | $ 0 | $ 18,000,000 | 0.0% |
| SUBTOTAL 7000 CONTINGENCY | $ 43,126,909 | $ 0 | $ 43,126,909 | $ 0 | $ 43,126,909 | |
| PROJECT TOTALS | $ 385,000,000 | $ 21,544,041 | $ 363,455,959 | $ 2,600,638 | $382,399,362 | 0.7% |

# Master Program Schedule Sample

KLMK group

| ID | Task Name | Start | Finish |
|---|---|---|---|
| 1 | Hospital One - New Hospital Project | Thu 5/1/08 | Thu 7/4/13 |
| 2 | | | |
| 3 | Strategic Plan Phase | Thu 5/1/08 | Fri 11/28/08 |
| 4 | Development of Strategic Plan | Thu 5/1/08 | Fri 8/29/08 |
| 6 | Complete Strategic Master Facilities Plan | Mon 9/1/08 | Fri 11/28/08 |
| 8 | | | |
| 9 | Project Launch Phase | Mon 12/1/08 | Tue 3/31/09 |
| 10 | Launch Gap Analysis | Mon 12/1/08 | Fri 2/27/09 |
| 12 | Project Implementation Plan | Mon 3/2/09 | Tue 3/31/09 |
| 14 | | | |
| 15 | Design Phase | Tue 2/24/09 | Mon 2/28/11 |
| 16 | Integrated Process Planning | Wed 4/1/09 | Mon 11/30/09 |
| 18 | Functional & Space Programming | Wed 4/8/09 | Fri 7/17/09 |
| 29 | Master Planning | Tue 4/28/09 | Mon 8/31/09 |
| 43 | Technology Design | Wed 5/6/09 | Fri 7/31/09 |
| 50 | Materials Management / Supply Chain Design | Mon 6/15/09 | Wed 9/30/09 |
| 59 | Medical Equipment Planning | Wed 6/10/09 | Mon 11/30/09 |
| 66 | Preconstruction | Wed 4/8/09 | Mon 5/31/10 |
| 75 | Permitting/Impact Studies | Fri 3/27/09 | Fri 3/26/10 |
| 102 | Civil Design Production | Tue 2/24/09 | Mon 3/1/10 |
| 113 | Architectural Design Production | Mon 9/14/09 | Mon 2/28/11 |
| 134 | Structural / Site Design Production | Tue 12/15/09 | Fri 7/2/10 |
| 143 | | | |
| 144 | Construction Phase | Tue 3/2/10 | Fri 2/8/13 |
| 145 | Earthwork | Tue 3/2/10 | Fri 8/13/10 |
| 146 | Foundations | Mon 7/19/10 | Fri 10/15/10 |
| 147 | Superstructure | Mon 9/27/10 | Fri 7/29/11 |
| 148 | Fit-Out | Mon 7/4/11 | Fri 12/14/12 |
| 149 | Certificate-of-Occupancy | Fri 12/14/12 | Fri 12/14/12 |
| 150 | Trim & Polish | Mon 12/17/12 | Fri 2/8/13 |
| 151 | | | |
| 152 | Transition and Occupancy Phase | Mon 4/12/10 | Thu 7/4/13 |
| 153 | Transition Readiness Assessment | Mon 4/12/10 | Fri 7/30/10 |
| 154 | Transition Implementation Plan | Mon 7/19/10 | Fri 9/17/10 |
| 155 | Management & Monitoring | Mon 9/20/10 | Mon 12/17/12 |
| 156 | Final FF&E Installation, Training, Physical Move | Mon 12/17/12 | Fri 3/29/13 |
| 157 | Patient Move | Sun 3/31/13 | Sun 3/31/13 |
| 158 | Post Occupancy & Closeout | Sun 3/31/13 | Thu 7/4/13 |

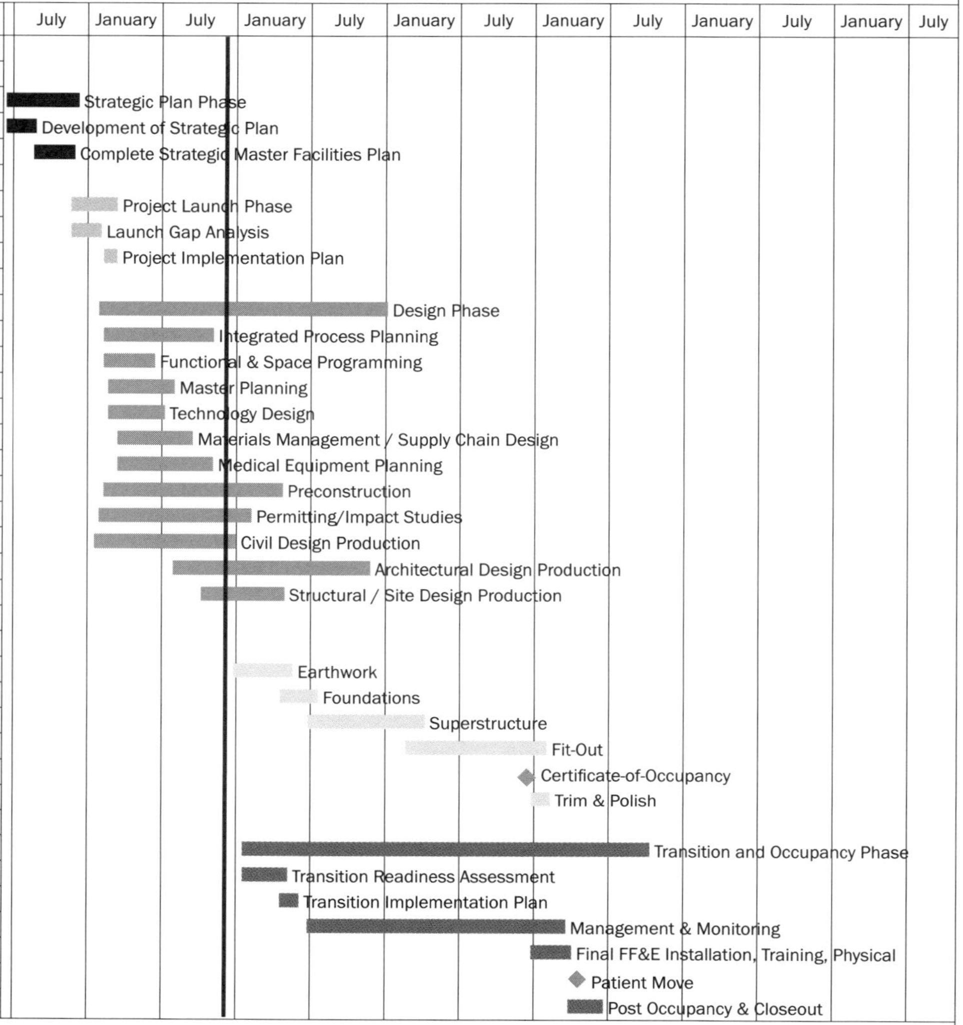

Client: HOSONE

Project: New Hospital Project

Legend: Strategic Plan Phase — Design Phase — Project Launch Phase — Milestone — Construction Phase — Transition & Occupancy Phase

Timeline header (repeating): July · January · July · January · July · January · July · January · July · January · July · January · July

# Acknowledgments

This second edition was made possible by many people in the healthcare industry. First, I would to like to thank Eileen Lynch and all the fine people at Health Administration Press. Eileen recognized the need for a second edition even with the slowdown of capital projects, and the staff made it easy to produce this book.

Second, I am grateful to all of our clients over the years. They gave our firm the opportunity to lead the delivery of their projects, and the lessons and experience we gained from those projects form the foundation of this book. As was the case with the first edition, our long-term clients have been instrumental in this book's development: Lyle Sheldon, FACHE, president and CEO of Upper Chesapeake Health in Bel Air, Maryland; Bill Flannagan, FACHE, executive vice president at Potomac Hospital in Woodbridge, Virginia; Rodger Baker, president and CEO of Fauquier Hospital in Warrenton, Virginia; Darrell Cutts, CEO of Piedmont Fayette Community Hospital in Fayetteville, Georgia; and Chet Kaletkowski, FACHE, president and CEO of South Jersey Health in Bridgeton, New Jersey. Special thanks for the vision to implement integrated project delivery on their projects goes to Jody Burdell, COO of Children's National Medical Center in Washington, DC; Greg Strahan, COO of Owensboro Medical Health System in Owensboro, Kentucky; and Jamal Ghani, senior vice president for Operations of Hurley Medical Center in Flint, Michigan. I thank all of them for having the confidence in our people to entrust the success of their capital projects to our firm.

Third, many of my colleagues contributed to this book through their fine work. I would especially like to thank my partner, Bill McMahon; Patrick Duke and Curtis Skolnick, who contributed a great deal this book; and all the current employees of KLMK Group, LLC. Each and every day, these people are dedicated to perfecting the delivery process for the benefit of healthcare organizations. They are an amazing group of people.

Lastly, I would like to thank my wife, Deborah. She tolerated my spending many weekends writing this book, but more important, she served as my "shadow" editor. Without her help, I would not have been able to complete this endeavor.

# About the Author

John E. Kemper is the founding partner and chairman/CEO of KLMK Group, LLC, a leading national client advisory firm specializing in healthcare, based in Richmond, Virginia. Mr. Kemper has more than 40 years of experience in all aspects of facilities development. For the past 20 years, he has worked exclusively for healthcare providers across the United States and in other countries. Prior to founding KLMK Group, Mr. Kemper served as president and COO of W.R. Adams Company, Inc., a leading national project management firm. He has also worked for a large architectural and engineering firm and an international construction management company.

Mr. Kemper's consulting work focuses on assisting healthcare organizations launch and manage capital facilities projects. In the past ten years, he has been involved in projects that have a total value of more than $18 billion.

Mr. Kemper is a member of the American College of Healthcare Executives, and an affiliate member of the Center for Healthcare Design and the National Association of Children's Hospitals and Related Institutions. He is a member of the Board of Directors for the International Hospital for Children and a contributing author of *The Latest Thinking: Project Delivery Strategies for Healthcare Buildings*. Mr. Kemper earned a bachelor of science in civil engineering from Virginia Military Institute. He can be reached at jkemper@klmkgroup. com, and his firm's website is www.klmkgroup.com.